SEATTLE
WALKS

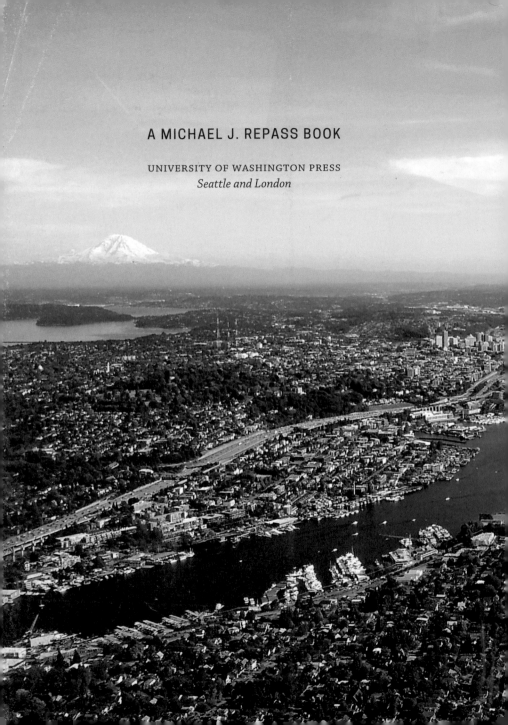

A MICHAEL J. REPASS BOOK

UNIVERSITY OF WASHINGTON PRESS
Seattle and London

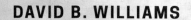

DAVID B. WILLIAMS

Seattle Walks

DISCOVERING HISTORY
AND NATURE IN THE CITY

Seattle Walks was published with the assistance of a grant from the Michael J. Repass Book Fund, which supports publications about the history and culture of Washington, Oregon, and Idaho.

Additional support was provided by the Northwest Writers Fund, which promotes the work of some of the region's most talented nonfiction writers and was established through generous gifts from Linda and Peter Capell, Janet and John Creighton, Michael J. Repass, and other donors.

UNIVERSITY OF WASHINGTON PRESS
www.washington.edu/uwpress

LIBRARY OF CONGRESS CATALOGING-IN-PUBLICATION DATA

Names: Williams, David B., 1965– author.
Title: Seattle walks : discovering history and nature in the city / David B. Williams.
Description: Seattle : University of Washington Press, [2017] | "A Michael J. Repass Book." | Includes bibliographical references and index.
Identifiers: LCCN 2016036152 | ISBN 9780295741284 (Paperback : acid-free paper)
Subjects: LCSH: Walking—Washington (State)—Seattle Metropolitan Area—Guidebooks. | Natural history—Washington (State)—Seattle Metropolitan Area. | Natural resources—Washington (State)—Seattle Metropolitan Area. | Urban geology—United States. | Seattle Metropolitan Area (Wash.)—Guidebooks.
Classification: LCC GV199.42.W22 S429 2017 | DDC 917.97/77204—dc23
LC record available at https://lccn.loc.gov/2016036152

The paper used in this publication is acid-free and meets the minimum requirements of American National Standard for Information Sciences—Permanence of Paper for Printed Library Materials, ANSI Z39.48–1984. ∞

To Scott and Muff,
great friends on all
of life's adventures

0   1   2 Miles

N

Shilshole Bay

Discovery Park

Green Lake

NE Northgate Way

Holman Rd NW

NW 85th St

15th Ave NW

NW 65th St

NW Market St

N 45th St

NE 65th St

NE 45th St

Roosevelt Way NE

NE 95th St

Sand Point Way NE

W Nickerson St

15th Ave W

Elliott Ave W

Denny Way

Elliott Bay

HARBOR ISLAND

W SEATTLE BRIDGE

SW Admiral Way

Fauntleroy Way SW

Delridge Way SW

Broadway

Yesler Way

23rd Ave E

24th Ave E

Madison St

Lake Washington Blvd

Lake Washington

Rainier Ave S

15th Ave S

Beacon Ave S

Duwamish Waterway

Rainier Ave S

Seward Park

MER ISLA

INSET MAP FOR DOWNTOWN WALKS

CONTENTS

ACKNOWLEDGMENTS

One of the pleasures of writing is to experience the generosity of strangers, colleagues, and friends who provide help in myriad and marvelous ways: Tony Angell, Aggeliki Barberopoulou, Linda Beaumont, Knute Berger, Emily Bishton, Morgan Blanchard, Derek Booth, Marta Brace, Deborah Brown, Fred Brown, John Buswell, George Comstock, Susan Connole, Barbara De-Caro, Ben Dittbrenner, Ron Edge, Lynn Ferguson, Rebecca Frestedt, David Giblin, John Gomes, Andrew Hedden, Jim Hensley, Arthur Lee Jacobson, Lezlie Jane, Lorna Jordan, Hollye Keister, Rob Ketcherside, Bob Kovalenko, Kate Krafft, Lissa Kramer, Bill Laprade, Mira Latoszek, Carolyn Law, Chris Leman, Katherine Lynch, Betsy Lyons, Karen Meador, Pete Mills, Joji Mina-togawa, Miye Moriguchi, Liz Nesbitt, Doan Nguyen, Ken North, Bridget Nowlin, Cass O'Callaghan, Jeffrey Ochsner, Dennis Paulson, Joan Peter-son, Kevin Peterson, Tom Redman, Steve Richmond, Joe Rocchio, Craig Romano, Anna Rudd, Jim Sander, Aurora Santiago, Colleen Schaforth, Allison Schwartz, Nancy Seasholes, Andy Sheffer, Amir Sheikh, Mimi Sheridan, Pete Spalding, Joe Starstead, Rainier Storb, Woody Sullivan, Ty Swenson, Paul Talbert, Nile Thompson, Kathy Troost, Patrick Trotter, Dave Tucker, Dick Wagner, Natasha Walicki, Eric Warner, Monica Wooton, Virginia Wright, Michael Yadrick, MariLyn Yim, Lizzie Zemke, and Gary Zimmerman.

I was very fortunate to have a host of people who tested these walks. Any remaining errors or poor directions are certainly not due to their thought-ful advice and suggestions: Paula Becker, Judy Bentley, Marty Bixler, Aaron Brackney, Barry Brown, Sandy Chalk, Melissa Coiley, Nancy Day, Roxanne Everett, Samantha Everett, Howie Frumkin, Brad Frye, Sarah Gage, Eldan Goldenberg, Carolyn Heberlein, Regan Huff, Kirk Johnson, Whitney John-son, Casey LaVela, Tom Lowndes, Gary Luke, Jessie McClurg, Shauna Mc-Daniel, Tom Meyer, Nicole Mitchell, Jeff Moline, Gail Neuenschwander, Wes Neuenschwander, Lynn Olson, Steve Olson, Whitney Rearick, Melanie

Reed, Trapper Robbins, Kale Rose, Anna Roth, Joyce Rudolph, Laura Sammons, Stephanie Seibert, Fran Siciliano, Arne Simon, Peter Stekel, Jeff Wall, Alberta Weinberg, and Lizzie White.

Thanks to the archivists and librarians who gave me such great support and assistance: Ann Ferguson (Seattle Public Library), Anne Frantilla (City of Seattle Archives), Ken House (National Archives), Anne Jenner (University of Washington Special Collections), Julie Kerssen (City of Seattle Archives), Greg Lange (King County Archives), Gary Lundell (University of Washington Special Collections), Carolyn Marr (Museum of History and Industry), Dean Noble (Seattle Public Utilities Engineering Archives), Carla Rickerson (University of Washington Special Collections), and Jordan Wong (Wing Luke Museum of the Asian Pacific American Experience).

Thanks to my pals in the Unspeakables and to Carol Doig for your generosity of spirit and on-going friendship.

Thanks to 4Culture for financial support.

Thanks to Judy Bentley and Laurence Kreissman for your careful, diligent, and thorough reviews of my manuscript.

Thanks to the University of Washington Press for your continued support: Tom Eykemans (once again, your design is stunning), Whitney Johnson, Casey LaVela, Rachael Levay, Nicole Mitchell, and Jacqueline Volin. Thanks to Kate Hoffman for her careful and thoughtful copyediting. And another big thanks to my favorite editor, Regan Huff. I said it on the last book and it still applies—you rock!

And my final thanks to my wife, Marjorie, who has been my constant partner on all of my best walks in life.

SEATTLE
WALKS

INTRODUCTION

> Walkers are "practitioners of the city," for the city is made to be
> walked, [Michael de Certeau] wrote. A city is a language, a repository
> of possibilities, and walking is the act of speaking that language, of
> selecting from those possibilities.
> —Rebecca Solnit, *Wanderlust: A History of Walking*

I may be odd, but I look forward to Seattle's long winters when the weather
is mild and the mountains full of snow, for it gives me no excuse not to do
one of my favorite urban activities: exploring Seattle on foot. For the past
15 years or so, my wife and I have strolled through most of the city, sometimes alone, often with friends. Our plan is usually simple—pick a spot on
the map and see what we can discover—but we also set goals, such as going
from one bakery to another, following some old map I have unearthed, or
seeing how far we can travel on the shoreline at low tide. We have almost
always had fun, often in ways we did not expect.

Each of these adventures has revealed some new facet of the city. Spectacular and little known viewpoints on Beacon Hill. Two-hundred-foot-tall
Douglas firs in Schmitz Park. An unexpected Civil War cemetery on Capitol
Hill. A secret bunker on Pigeon Point. An amazing taco truck in Rainier
Beach. The house where Elvis once slept near Alki Point. (The walks in the
book pass by all of these locations.) Urban walking is simply the best way to
get to know a place and to develop deeper connections to its story.

In addition, there are some wonderful advantages to urban walking
compared to wilderness hiking. (I am not saying that one is better than the
other; I recommend both.) You can complete an urban walk after dinner.
Your carbon footprint is smaller because you don't have to drive as far. Better yet, you can bike or bus to the walk. (Both means of transportation are
also great ways to discover the city; several of my suggested walks are one

way with a return by bus.) You can go on an urban walk any day of the year. Urban provisions are generally better, or if you simply get hungry, a meal is not too far away. If it's raining, you can always duck in somewhere and dry out. You can go with friends of all ages.

Walking with friends has also led me to taking out groups. I have explored Seattle with elementary school kids, with my mom's Walkie Talkie gang (average age 75 plus), and with employees of the Washington Trails Association. I have also led guided walks for many organizations from the Burke Museum to the Seattle Audubon Society. The two most common comments I hear: "Wow, I've walked by here a thousand times and never noticed that" and "I will never look at that building the same again."

These guided walks are one of the reasons I decided to write *Seattle Walks*. I wanted to be able to share these walks with more people and reveal what I have discovered on the ground. I also wanted a place to share my inner geek. Many of my discoveries in the field, such as the dozens of carved faces on a downtown building (which make me wonder who the models were) or the nuclear fallout shelter under Interstate 5 near Green Lake, have inspired me to head to an archive to scroll through microfiche, read old letters, or pore over maps in hopes of discovering the story behind what I have seen. Each discovery is a little mystery to solve. One of the great pleasures of living in Seattle is that it is easy to access so many of the primary documents of our history.

The walks are also an outgrowth of two of my previous books: *The Seattle Street-Smart Naturalist: Field Notes from the City* and *Too High and Too Steep: Reshaping Seattle's Topography*. In each of these books, I tried to bring the reader with me as I explored the human and natural history of Seattle. In *Seattle Walks*, I wanted to take my research and the stories I wrote about previously—the regrading of Denny Hill, restoration along Thornton Creek, and the 3.5-billion-year-old stone that clads a downtown building— and create easy-to-follow routes that encourage people to get out in the field, see and experience what I have been writing about, and perhaps follow up with their own research when questions arise.

As for selecting a walk, I encourage you to venture into new parts of Seattle and discover the diversity of terrains, people, cultures, and green spaces that make up the city. One of the simple pleasures of walking is getting out of one's routine. In respect to areas I don't address, they are locales that are already well covered in other books.

I also suggest you try some of the longer walks. I have friends who have said that a five-mile urban walk feels longer than a five-mile hike in the woods. I disagree, but if you find this to be true for you, I suggest you break the walk into two parts, walk more slowly, or take more breaks (which provides an excuse to try every coffee shop on the walk). I have taken friends on the longer walks, so I know that these can be done by most people, and my companions did have fun.

Ultimately, I hope that these walks will enable you to see Seattle in a new light and to acquire a new appreciation for how the city has changed through time, how the past influences the present, and how nature is all around us, even in the urban landscape, which many people consider the least wild place around. And I trust that you will make many discoveries on your own.

PRACTICAL MATTERS

My Philosophy

I am generally not a goal oriented person, but some of these walks have a distinct goal, namely, to get you from a particular geographic feature to another. One such example is the Madison Street walk, which goes from Elliott Bay to Lake Washington. Madison is the only street in Seattle where you can do this without any zigs, zags, or breaks. Because of my desire to make geographic connections, some walks have long distances between stops. I did this on purpose; I could have pointed out every interesting building or tree or curious feature along the way, but I chose not to. I hope you will use the time between points of interest to consider what you have seen, to make your own observations, or to simply walk along and enjoy being outside.

How the Book Is Organized

The book begins with walks in the city center; later walks form a clockwise spiral around the city center. Except for the Madison Street walk, each of the downtown walks is less than two miles long. There are so many downtown walks because each covers a different theme—geology, geography, regrades, and architectural motifs—in a manner that reveals the complexities of a city and how one place can have many stories. Central walks also include the Regrades and International District walk, which is easily accessible from downtown, and the Madison Street walk, which begins downtown. The circumnavigation of Lake Union follows because it's also close to downtown. Subsequent walks head to the neighborhoods starting north of downtown with Magnolia, then east toward Lake Washington, south to south Seattle, and ultimately conclude in West Seattle.

What to Bring

I tend to carry a backpack where I can stash a rain jacket, extra food, a water bottle, and perhaps a coffee mug, binoculars, magnifying lens, and notebook and paper. I also wear a hat and bring sun block. Now that most people carry smart phones, I figure you have a camera with you, but if not, one might be a nice addition to the urban walk essentials.

How to Use This Book

Each walk consists of six parts:

- Basic information: a title, a one-sentence description, details about length and starting and ending points, and notes on public transportation, restrooms, and/or terrain.
- A map of the route showing the locations of numbered highlights.
- Directions to specific numbered locations, where you should stop and read the description. On a few walks, the directions don't take you to a specific location, but take you instead past several intriguing spots. These walks include a statement such as "Consider the following as you walk." In these cases, there will be information about what and where the number refers to on the map.
- Descriptions about the natural and human history.
- Sidebars with additional information about subjects that might be covered in several walks, side trips, or supplemental details about a particular feature.
- Source material at the end of the book with references for further research.

In addition, be aware of the following:

- All walks are on pavement unless otherwise noted.
- Walks are roundtrip loops unless otherwise noted.
- On the one-way downtown walks (1, 4, and 5), I don't provide directions on how to return to the start because there are numerous bus

routes that you can take or the walk is short enough that you can return by foot. One-way walks that are not downtown (7, 10, and 15) end where you have the option of returning by Metro bus. For information on bus service, go to http://metro.kingcounty.gov/.

- I have attempted to make the routes as flat as possible, and I will note if there are hills.
- In the downtown walks, directions are expressed using north, east, south, and west instead of the more navigationally correct northwest, northeast, southeast, southwest. These simplified directions are more commonly used.
- Many of the walks pass through areas with numerous businesses, where one can take advantage of their amenities, including public restrooms. On walks through neighborhoods where restrooms are harder to find, I note the location of public facilities.
- Regarding dogs, they are allowed on all walks, including the ones in parks and other green spaces. Dogs must be leashed, and you need to pick up after them. I am not sure though how much dogs would enjoy the downtown walks as green space is scant and people and cars are many.
- I return to several topics regularly throughout the book. These include glacial geology, Seattle's Great Fire, the Lake Washington Ship Canal, and regrading. To help readers navigate these topics, I have included cross-references to other walks that offer additional details about the subject.
- Seattle is a dynamic city where change is constant. I have tried to write with this in mind. If you come across some feature that is new, if a bus route has changed, or if a feature or detail I describe no longer exists, I ask that you remember that change is part of what makes Seattle an interesting (and yes, sometimes annoying) place to live.
- Please use common sense when you are out walking. Seattle is a large city and has the corresponding challenges that make some neighborhoods less safe than others. If you encounter people, animals, weather, or anything that makes you feel uncomfortable or unsafe, leave or go another way; the walk can always be done another time. And please do obey traffic laws.
- By all means, have fun.

Seattle's Historic Shoreline

REMNANTS FROM THE PAST

Trace the original shoreline of downtown Seattle
to see clues that reveal its modern form.

DISTANCE	1.5 miles, one way
STARTING POINT	Alaskan Way and Lenora Street
ENDING POINT	Occidental Park, Occidental Avenue S and S Main Street
NOTES	The walk has one ascent of 67 steps, which gains about 55 feet.

Like many cities built on the water, Seattle has drastically changed its historic footprint. In particular, some of the greatest alteration has occurred along Elliott Bay, where bluffs have been reduced, beaches eliminated, and shorelines pushed out into the water. The latter process is known as "making land," when material is dumped into the water to raise the ground surface from below sea level to above.

Along the historic shoreline covered in this walk, railroads primarily drove the building of new land. The reason was simple: The railroads needed a way to access the downtown business district, and the best means was not over the hills that surround Elliott Bay but around their base. What

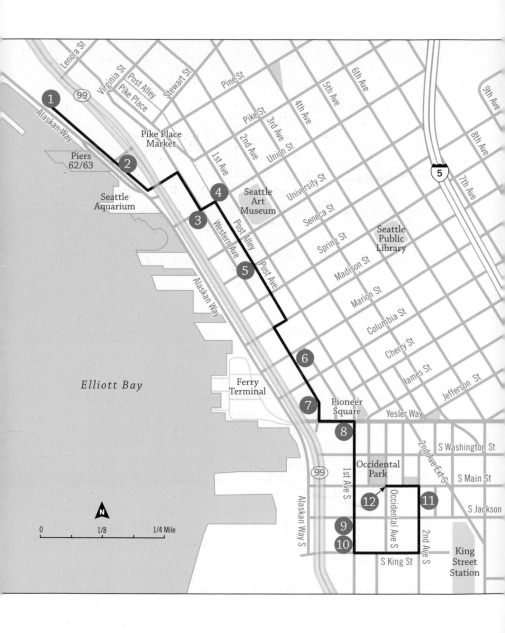

Railroad Avenue, looking north from Madison Street (no date)

started as a single wooden trestle carrying one train line over the shallow water along the shoreline grew into a system of interconnected trestles known as Railroad Avenue.

By 1905, nine sets of tracks wove across Railroad Avenue. It was a dangerous place; at least 10 people died in train accidents in one two-year period. Nor was it safe under the trestles, which became a dumping ground for garbage favored by rats, many of which carried fleas that harbored plague. In 1907, two people died from pneumonic plague and one from bubonic plague. A 1936 report concluded that improved sanitary conditions such as rebuilding the waterfront helped prevent the spread of plague.

Engineers eventually realized that they needed to fill in the area around the trestles to create a more stable surface for trains, as well as for automobiles and pedestrians. This led to two periods of construction of a seawall, during 1916 and from 1934 to 1936. When it was completed, the city changed the name Railroad Avenue to Alaskan Way.

Since the founding of Seattle in the early 1850s, approximately 2,800 acres of new land (about five times more land than Discovery Park) has been made. This includes Interbay, along the waterfront, and across the tideflats of the Duwamish River. Although the original historic shoreline has long been buried, many indicators remain that help reveal its former location.

In addition to tracing the historic shoreline of downtown Seattle, this walk includes stops at an unusual source of heat for downtown buildings, Seattle's most infamous lost ship, and one of the city's earliest houses of ill-repute.

Start on the east side of Alaskan Way at Lenora Street (2000 Alaskan Way). Look at the bluff that rises to the east behind the fence and under the overpass.

❶ Before you rises a unique hillside, the last remaining bluff in downtown Seattle. Historically, steep faces of sand and silt wrapped around Elliott Bay. Now all but this one are gone, at least on the downtown side of the bay; the rest disappeared under the advances of urban development.

Imagine yourself here in 1850, just before the first European settlers arrived. You would have been standing on the shoreline. A high bluff such as this one would have continued south, slowly losing elevation toward what is now Pioneer Square. At the base of the bluff would have been a narrow sand shelf, or ledge, covered in trees fallen from above and logs washed in by storms. The shelf dropped down to a beach of sand and rocks, which sloped gently out to the water. At high tide, waves would have pushed up to the base of the ledge, and at low tide, a sandy beach would have extended out into the water. The best nearby example of this is West Point at Discovery Park in the Magnolia neighborhood.

Another way to consider this landscape is to realize that most of the land west of the fence did not exist in 1850. It is all made land, created primarily by the building of Seattle's original seawall and the filling in of the area behind it with sediment. But as we will see, early Seattleites also made new land by dumping what could best be described as garbage.

Walk south on Alaskan Way on the Elliott Bay Trail to Pine Street (next intersection). Watch out for bicyclists and other wheeled travelers.

❷ If this were low tide in 1850, you would be standing 20 feet lower on a beach of coarse sand, rounded pebbles, small cobbles, broken shells, and a smattering of woody debris. Evidence of that beach still exists: in 2012 a seven-inch-wide column cored here revealed gray sediments from that earlier time.

THE GREAT NORTHERN TUNNEL

Built by James J. Hill for his Great Northern Railroad, the tunnel runs for 5,141 feet under Seattle. It begins just north of Pine Street, behind the large buildings on Alaskan Way, and emerges at 4th Avenue S and S Washington Street, just north of King Street Station, or what was originally known as the Union Depot.

Crews started work from opposite ends of the tunnel in April 1903, using picks, shovels, and wheelbarrows. The two tunnels became one 125 feet below ground on October 26, 1904. Along the way, the tunneling teams encountered a forest of petrified trees, underground springs, and an old streambed. They also had a few troubles, including buildings settling as the tunnel extended beneath them. One of the structures, the York Hotel, at 1st Avenue and Pike Street, sustained so much damage that the Great Northern bought it and leveled it. Workers completed the tunnel in January 1905.

If you get a chance to see the tunnel entrances, note the notches cut into the archways. They were added in the 1980s to facilitate double-stack container trains, which needed the extra room. The tunnel is now used by BNSF and Amtrak trains.

At the time it was built, Seattleites jokingly called it the longest tunnel in the world, because it ran from Virginia (Street) to Washington (Street). Such was humor in the early 20th century.

The core was drilled as part of the archaeological studies for the replacement of the historic seawall. Cores were taken along the entire stretch of wall from S Washington Street in the south to Broad Street in the north. Because the sediments are soft, drillers used a roto-sonic drill, which not only spins but also vibrates 100 to 200 times a second. The oscillating drill parts cause the surrounding sediments to lose cohesion and liquefy, allowing for rapid penetration of the drill casing—a high-strength steel tube—into the ground. For the archaeological work, workers drilled out seven-inch-wide cores in 10 foot-long sections. The long core from this location contains about 20 feet of fill that was piled upon beach deposits. At the top are a couple of inches of concrete, followed by 6 inches of gravel, 11 feet of sand, 2 more feet of gravel, 4 feet of silt, and finally a foot of mostly sand with scattered bits of wood. *Sand* and *gravel* are misleading terms, because the content of those layers is not pure. Cores from this area generally contain garbage dumped by the city's early inhabitants, including glass and brick fragments, sawdust, cinders, slag, charcoal, plaster, rubber, leather, bone, and concrete. This is typical of cores found all along the waterfront, at least closest to the original shoreline. Closer to the seawall is where most of the sediment was dumped.

Continue south on the trail to Pike Street, turn left, or east, and walk to the Pike Street Hillclimb. Ascend the 67 stairs to Western Avenue (the first street you encounter), turn right, or south, and walk to Union Street.

❸ You are now back at the historic shoreline. The 400 feet of land between this point and the seawall to the west is all made land. Also note the elevation change between this point and 1st Avenue (at the top of the wall due east of you) and the additional drop to Alaskan Way, west of you. To reach sea level, you would have to drop another 10 to 20 feet. If you stood at this point in 1850, you would have been on a beach about 35 to 50 feet lower than you are now, with a 70- to 80-foot-high bluff rising above you. That is why no road unites downtown with the waterfront at Union Street.

Walk east on Union Street to where it dead-ends at Post Alley.

❹ For the next few blocks, the historic shoreline runs south down Post Alley. The name came from a post office that opened in June 1880 at the corner of what was then Mill Street, now Yesler Way, and an alley that intersected the street. Originally a dirt road, Post was covered in wood planks in the late 1880s and, in 1910, with paving atop 8 to 14 feet of compacted sand, gravel, and cinders. By this time, although functioning as an alley, Post Alley had earned the name Post Street or Post Avenue.

The nearby industrial-looking buildings with the chimneys and gray tower house the Seattle Steam plant.

Turn right and walk south down Post Alley to Seneca Street.

❺ At Seneca, Post Alley changes its name to Post Avenue. This is the last point on the walk where a street trending east–west does not connect 1st Avenue to the waterfront. South of here, the bluffs, or sand banks, were no longer too high to block roads from being built down to the water.

Historically, there was a break in the bluff line at Seneca. According to J. Willis Sayre's somewhat whimsical guide to early-day Seattle, *This City of*

Ours, a bridge on what was Front Street and is now 1st Avenue once crossed Seneca at this spot. Below the bridge, a ravine provided access for traffic to go from the beach up to 2nd Avenue. South of the ravine to Madison, wrote Sayre, ran "high banks of dirt on the left-hand side and an abrupt drop-off to the beach on the right-hand side."

Continue south on Post Avenue two blocks until it ends at Madison Street. You are now slightly west of the historic shoreline, which ran down what was known as Front Street (now 1st Avenue). Turn right, or west, walk to Western Avenue, and turn left, or south, and walk to Marion Street.

⑥ On December 30, 1875, the 161-foot-long, three-masted bark *Windward* was carrying a load of lumber to San Francisco when she ran aground in the fog in Whidbey Island's Useless Bay. Because her owner owed wealthy Seattle entrepreneur James Colman $800, Colman acquired the ruined ship and had it towed to Seattle, where it was beached on the shorefront. By the late 1880s, the ship had become a husk, with all valuables stripped away and no masts. When a new railroad trestle was built along the waterfront, the builders simply plowed right through the *Windward*, driving piles as they went.

Unfortunately, we do not know the bark's exact location. Speculation had long placed the *Windward* under a parking lot on Western between Marion and Columbia, but no evidence of the ship was found during excavation of the Post apartments, which replaced the parking lot in 2012. Archaeologists who worked on that project suspect that the *Windward* lies due north–south in the middle of the block, with its northern end extending into Western Avenue and the rest buried under a building on the west side of Western.

Continue south on Western, past Columbia, until the road bends slightly, next to a large brick building.

⑦ The brick buildings next to you are part of Enwave Seattle, formerly known as Seattle Steam. Established the year after Seattle's Great Fire of 1889 so that businesses could avoid housing coal-fired boilers, which increased the risk of fire, Seattle Steam burned coal to make steam that could be sent by pipes to heat nearby buildings. It also provided pressurized water to run hydraulic elevators, as well as electricity for downtown streetcars.

Over the years Seattle Steam expanded to four buildings. The two at this end of Western were built in 1890 and 1902 and had 11 coal-fired boilers. For decades a dominant sight along the waterfront was the company's 70-foot-tall chimney spewing nasty black smoke. The third and fourth buildings, at Western and Union Streets, are now the company's principal suppliers of steam, which is produced by natural gas and renewable biomass, or waste wood.

Seattle Steam continues to send steam for heat to more than 200 buildings across downtown and up to First Hill. These include hotels, which use reclaimed water from its steam for laundry; hospitals, which sterilize medical instruments with its steam; the Seattle Art Museum, which relies on its steam for precise humidity control for sensitive artwork; and businesses that require steam for their own sensitive products, such as beer and cheese.

To reach these buildings, the steam travels through more than 18 miles of pipes. It is not the ordinary steam that we see coming out of our teakettles. That "steam" is actually condensed droplets of water vapor. Seattle Steam's steam is a clear gas heated to 320 degrees and flowing at up to 250 pounds of pressure. If the steam traveled through a clear pipe, you would not be able to see it.

You have most likely seen a by-product of the steam pipes, however. Despite the high pressure and temperature, a small amount of water trickles within the pipes, which can lead to what is known as water hammer, or propagating pressure waves that can cause the pipes to explode. Plant operators combat water hammer by regularly draining the pipes, resulting in heated water that periodically vents as "steam" through hatch covers.

Continue south on Western until it intersects Yesler Way. (This was about the location of Seattle's first large business, Henry Yesler's sawmill.) Turn left, or east, and walk two blocks to 1st Avenue.

❸ You have reached the geographic heart of early-day Seattle, the area where the first settlers decided to establish their town. It is also an area of great importance to the Native people who lived and continue to live here. The Little Crossing-Over Place, or *sdZéédZul7aleecH* in Whulshootseed, refers to a trail either to a nearby lagoon or over to Lake Washington. When the settlers arrived here in 1852, they found the ruins of three longhouses.

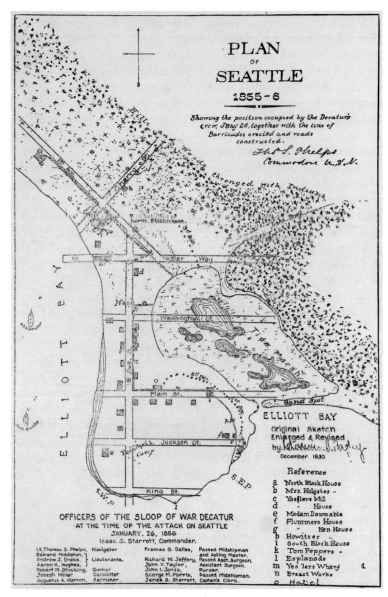

1930 modification of Thomas Phelps's 1856 map of Seattle

Historically, this area was known as the Neck (1st Avenue south from Yesler to just past S Washington Street), a reference to a sandbar that extended from the mainland to a peninsula that jutted south into Elliott Bay. The best place to see the Neck is on one of the most famous maps of Seattle. Drawn by Thomas Phelps, it depicts the young town in January 1856. Phelps was a lieutenant on the US sloop of war *Decatur,* which had arrived in Elliott Bay in October because of concerns about possible hostilities with the Native people. His map is the first to clearly show the human-built structures of Seattle and not just the landscape.

Atop the peninsula—known variously as the Point, Maynard's Point, and Denny's Island—were most of Seattle's residential houses. Behind the peninsula, which rose about 20 to 30 feet above sea level, was a tidal marsh or lagoon. The Point was not always connected to the mainland. At very high tides, water could flow over the Neck and convert the peninsula to an island, which led to the first land-making in Seattle, when a man named Dutch Ned filled a wheelbarrow with sawdust from Henry Yesler's mill and dumped it into the Neck. His goal was to raise the land high enough to prevent water from flowing over the Neck. The area around the mill eventually earned the name the Sawdust because of Dutch Ned's efforts.

Walk south on 1st Avenue S to S Jackson Street.

❾ For the past few blocks you have been traveling on what was Seattle's main street in 1856, about half a block east of the historic shoreline, which ran down what is now the alley west of 1st Avenue. The shoreline is now buried under you, as is the entire peninsula. One of the advantages of Seattle's Great Fire of 1889 and its destruction of the business district was that city planners could reengineer downtown streets, making them wider and more level. They accomplished this by adding fill to raise the streets up.

Near this intersection is the site of one of the more infamous buildings in Seattle's early history. Felker House, or Madam Damnable's, as some called it, was a two-story hotel that stood at the western edge of Maynard's Point overlooking Elliott Bay. Captain Leonard Felker had brought the prefabricated building to Seattle in the hold of his ship. The hotel's manager was Madam Damnable, who added to her income by running a brothel on the top floor. Also known as Mary Ann Conklin, she had arrived in Seattle

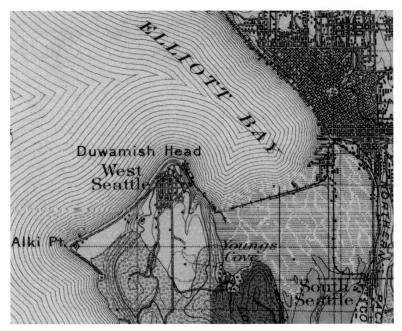

Elliott Bay, detail from an 1897 USGS map

in 1853 after her husband had abandoned her in Port Townsend, leaving her to survive by her own tenacity and determination. Her poetic name comes from her use of less than poetic language and, of course, her profession.

Walk south on 1st Ave S about three fourths of the block to the arched entrance to the Hambach Building.

⑩ This is roughly the southern edge of the former peninsula and the southernmost point in early-day Seattle. Imagine standing here in 1850— you would have been on a 20-foot-high bluff. To the south were the tideflats of the Duwamish River, which extended for about two and a half miles to the mouth of the river (about a half mile south of the modern-day Spokane Street overpass). To the east, the tideflats extended to the base of Beacon Hill, and to the west was the open water of Elliott Bay.

If the tide were in, you would have been surrounded by water, with waves breaking against the bluff below. At low tide, the tideflats would have been a landscape of mud, incised by numerous rivulets of the Du-wamish. Despite the lack of plant life, the abundance of birds, mammals, fish, and invertebrates made the tideflats an important food source for the Native people. The tideflats would also have been rather aromatic, as buried anaerobic bacteria consumed dead organic material and expelled pungent gases.

Continue to the end of the block, and at S King Street, turn left, or east, and walk two blocks to 2nd Avenue S. Turn left, or north, and walk about one and a half blocks until you are almost at the driveway of the fire station. *Please be aware that fire trucks may have to depart at any time.*

⑪ You have now made it around to what would have been the protected, or east, side of the peninsula, directly opposite the sand spit shown on the Phelps map. The spit would have extended almost to the peninsula and might have persisted for decades, allowing a feature such as a tidal marsh to form in the protected area behind the barrier.

Continue north on 2nd to S Main Street, turn left, or west, and walk over to Occidental Avenue S. Occidental Park is across the street.

⑫ In 1856, this would have been the center of the tidal marsh. We do not know the exact boundaries of the marsh—plus, they weren't fixed—but core samples taken in this area in 2007 provide some insight into where the marsh was and how early Seattleites eliminated it. Several cores contained layers of sawdust more than a foot deep, perhaps dumped by Dutch Ned. Others included layers of peat, which is what one would expect in a marsh, as well as brick, mortar, asphalt, cinders, concrete, lumber, and wood and charcoal debris.

As along the rest of the waterfront, Seattle's early settlers regularly dumped their waste materials around the old peninsula to make new land. This historic waste-disposal practice has led to some undesirable features in the modern built environment. A walk around Pioneer Square yields tilted sidewalks, alleys with undulating asphalt, sagging exterior walls held up by support rods, and foundations sunk below grade. All are the product of a less than stable subsurface that resulted from Seattleites' wholesale alter-ation of the landscape.

Despite these modern-day engineering challenges, the creation of usable land was critical to Seattle's growth as a city. It facilitated the development of railroad yards, opened up space for industry and manufacturing, and provided room for the expansion of maritime trade. We may not be able to physically see the historic shoreline of Seattle any longer, but we certainly still feel its effects and will continue to do so well into the future.

Denny Hill

THE BIG HILL THAT WENT AWAY

Circumnavigate the regrade district, focusing on
what the hill used to look like and what happened
once it was eliminated.

DISTANCE	1.9 miles
START/END	2nd Avenue and Pine Street
NOTES	Few places in Seattle have experienced greater change than this neighborhood, and change remains the norm today. Please be patient when you encounter new construction that affects the route.

Denny Hill once stood as the great barrier to progress in Seattle. At least that's how its opponents viewed the mound at the north end of downtown. The hill's steep south face prevented commerce from flowing "unhampered in its natural channels," wrote civic booster Welford Beaton. To Beaton and others such as city engineer R. H. Thomson, addressing this problem was critical to Seattle's future, and there was only one solution: the elimination, or regrading, of Denny Hill.

Leveling Denny required five separate regrades. The first lowered 1st Avenue in 1898. Five years later, work started on 2nd Avenue, and in 1906 it continued with the regrading of the south end of the hill. This regrade led to the destruction of the most famous building on Denny Hill: the grand six-story Washington Hotel (originally called the Denny Hotel). These first

◀ Denny Regrade, detail from Asahel Curtis photograph, May, 1910

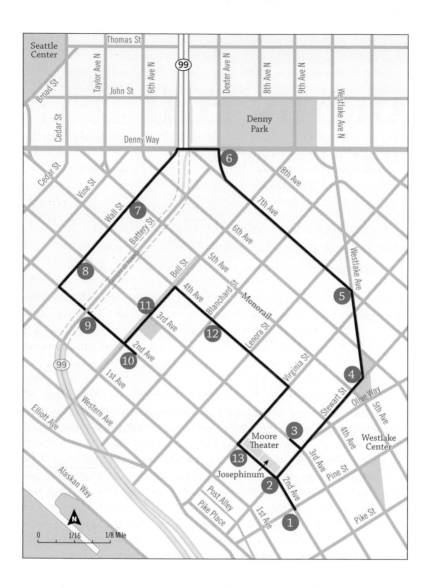

three regrades were all relatively small, totaling about 1.3 million cubic yards of sediment, most of which ended up in Elliott Bay.

What many refer to as Denny Regrade One (because it was the first of the two big regrades) took place from 1908 to 1911. As happened in the earlier regrades, but on a much grander scale, workers washed away the hill (I provide more details on the walk). And, once again, all of the sediment—5.4 million cubic yards—ended up in Elliott Bay. In contrast, workers on the fifth regrade, often called Denny Regrade Two (1928–30), used gasoline- and diesel-powered excavators to remove the hill. During the two years of work, conveyor belts transported 4.4 million cubic yards of sediment out to barges, which dumped the material in Elliott Bay. None of the sediment from any of the Denny regrades ended up in the Duwamish River's tideflats or in Harbor Island.

Start on the southwest corner of the intersection of 2nd Avenue and Pine Street.

❶ You are standing at the southwest corner of the former Denny Hill. Imagine standing at this intersection before the regrades. You would have been looking up the steepest face of the hill, which rose 100 feet to a high point at 3rd and Stewart. (As a comparison, the building on the southeast corner of 2nd and Pine rises 88 feet.) From that summit, the hill dropped slightly before rising north to a second high point, followed by a slope down to the north where the land leveled around Thomas Street, two blocks north of Denny Way. To the west, Denny Hill dropped steeply toward Elliott Bay, and to the east, it generally sloped more gently down into a valley, where Westlake Avenue now runs. Denny Hill topped out at 240 feet above sea level, less than half the heights of its neighbors, Queen Anne Hill and modern-day Capitol Hill.

I use the term *modern-day* because Denny Hill was originally called Capitol Hill, a reference to a short-lived plan by city founder Arthur Denny, who acquired the land in 1852, to donate 10 acres of his property for the state capitol. Although Denny's plan failed—in part because people thought that the hill was too far north of the main business district—about 50 houses dotted the landscape by 1878, and by 1884, most of the virgin forest had been logged. Not until 1889, when Arthur Denny and a group of investors began to build what they called the Denny Hotel, did the hill earn its permanent modern moniker.

Denny Regrade postcard. Note the use of hydaulic giants (white spray) and that the amount of dirt listed on the postcard is incorrect.

By the end of the 19th century, more than 360 homes, 70 multifamily dwellings, and a dozen apartment buildings covered Denny. Residents included many working-class people, who found the hill cheaper than the fashionable First and Queen Anne Hills. Other residents included many professionals and even a former mayor and city council member or two. Denny was close enough to downtown that residents could either walk there or ride one of the streetcar lines that skirted the hill.

Walk north on the west side of 2nd Avenue one block to Stewart Street.

❷ Across the street are two buildings that offer a convenient comparison with the former elevation of Denny Hill. Both buildings are associated with developer James Moore, who purchased the Denny Hotel from the initial investors. They had run out of money in 1893 and the mostly completed building sat empty until Moore purchased, completed, and opened it to the public, all in the first half of 1903. He also renamed it the Washington Hotel.

One of the most elegant hotels on the West Coast, Moore's Washington Hotel was open for only three years. In 1906, Moore agreed to have the property under his hotel regraded, which led to the hotel's destruction. Moore then sold part of his property to developers who built the New Washington, which became one of Seattle's premier hotels. It operated as a hotel until 1963 when the Catholic Archdiocese of Seattle purchased it, renamed it the Josephinum, and converted it to a residence for senior citizens. The 14-story building, which still retains the original marble foyer and staircases, is now low-income housing. It also houses the Christ Our Hope Catholic Church in the hotel's original dining room.

Moore's longer-lasting legacy is the Moore Theater and attached hotel (north end of block), which opened in 1907. Featuring marble and onyx, the foyer was called the largest of its kind in the country at the time.

To get a feel for the original height of Denny Hill, look to the top of the Moore Theater. It equals the hill's high point of 240 feet above sea level. Now look to the top of the Josephinum (across the street). It is about equal in elevation to what would have been the top of Moore's Washington Hotel. The vista from the old hotel, which towered above nearly every other building in the city and offered unimpeded views of the Cascades, Olympics, and Puget Sound, must have been spectacular.

Walk east on Stewart Street, cross 3rd Avenue, and turn left, or north, on the east side of 3rd. Walk up 3rd until you are across the street from a tan six-story building (1915 3rd Ave).

❸ To proponents of the regrade, the new, level land would create an ideal environment for businesses by providing customers and suppliers easy access to a new retail area adjacent to downtown. Few businesses, however, took advantage of the open space. One sector that did was the automobile industry in the form of parking lots, parking garages, gas stations, and repair shops. This is somewhat ironic considering that one reason for eliminating the hill was that it was too steep for horse-drawn vehicles to ascend, which was not a problem for cars.

By 1930, there were at least a dozen garages in the regrade area, most of which have now been converted to new uses or destroyed. One of the largest and most substantial was the White Garage across the street from you, which now holds storage units. Built in 1928 and designed by Henry Bittman (architect of the old Eagles Building, where the ACT building is now located on Walk 5), the garage originally had two lifts to take cars to parking spots on the higher floors. Most other garages were one or two stories.

On the southwest corner of 3rd and Stewart, note the terra-cotta building with the large display windows and bays, which characterized many of the automobile-related businesses.

Return back south to Stewart Street, turn left, or east, and continue to Westlake Avenue. Stay on the west side of the intersection. (Imagine doing the same walk in 1905. You would have lost 120 feet in elevation as you descended Stewart to Westlake, instead of the 45 feet you just dropped.)

❹ In 1905, a great upheaval occurred in this section of Seattle. After several years of discussions and planning, the city extended Westlake Avenue diagonally across the rectangular street grid from Denny Way to 4th Avenue and Pike Street (it now extends only to Stewart). Before the new construction, Westlake, or Rollin Avenue, as it was originally known, ran only north of Denny. Proponents hoped that the new thoroughfare would open up access to Lake Union and points north, which it did, primarily via streetcars that carried passengers along the same route as the modern South Lake Union Streetcar.

Imagine this spot when settlers first arrived. You would have been in a valley with a creek that flowed gently north toward Lake Union. To the east was a steep ascent, which was precipitous enough in January 1907 that seven horses died after sliding on the slope's icy roads. But you would not have been able to see this topography because of the forest. In 1855, for example, General Land Office (GLO) surveyors recorded an 80-inch-diameter Douglas fir, which probably typified the monster-size trees that covered the landscape. (The United States Congress passed the Land Ordinance of 1785, which established the GLO to survey and divide public land into townships that measured six miles square.)

Turn left, or north, and walk up the west side of Westlake to the corner of 7th Avenue. Across the street is a red-brick three-story building.

❺ Because of the new diagonal street, numerous buildings along Westlake have a triangular or angled footprint. In 1907, one of the first to be built was the brick building across the street, which formerly housed the Hotel Westlake. Many other odd-shaped buildings can still be found along Westlake and its historic route, particularly closer to downtown.

REGINALD HEBER THOMSON

No person was more responsible for Seattle's regrades than R. H. Thomson. Born in Indiana, he had been an unsuccessful mining engineer in California before arriving in Seattle in 1881. Three years later he became the city engineer, more or less inheriting the job from a cousin. To Thomson, Denny Hill was "an offense to the public." It blocked commerce, stifled transportation, and lowered land values. If Seattle wanted to grow as a city, it needed to somehow address the problematic hill, and the most feasible solution was regrading. By the time he left office in 1911 (he returned to the job again from 1930 to 1931 but had little influence), Thomson had orchestrated four regrades of Denny, as well as the regrades of Jackson Street and Dearborn Street. In addition, Thomson helped build new water and sewer systems for Seattle. He died in 1949, one year before his autobiography, *That Man Thomson*, was published.

Cross to the east side of 7th and walk north on 7th. After 7th curves to the right and becomes Dexter Avenue N, continue to the southeast corner of Denny Way and Dexter, directly across the street from Denny Park.

❻ David and Louisa Denny created Seattle's first cemetery when they donated part of their property near Lake Union to the city in 1864. Twenty years later the land became Seattle's first park—known as Seattle Park after the buried residents were moved up to what is now Volunteer Park. To honor the Dennys, the city changed the name of Seattle Park to Denny Park.

This is not the park's *true* first location; it was originally about 60 feet higher. During the final regrade of Denny Hill, George Cotterill, former mayor and assistant city engineer to R. H. Thomson, wanted to keep the park as a hill rising above the altered land below. "God's acre," as he called it, would be a "most beautiful and historic reminder of the pioneer era—the last of Denny Hill." In February 1930, the city council rejected Cotterill's idea and decided to lower the park to its present elevation. To compare the pre- and post-regrade elevations, consider the six-story building on the intersection's northwest corner, which is about 60 feet high.

Denny School, 1904

Walk west on Denny Way, veer left onto Wall Street, and continue west to the corner of 5th Avenue.

❼ Imagine standing at this intersection pre-regrade. You would find yourself next to one of Denny Hill's most beloved and beautiful buildings. Denny School was a two-story, wooden rectangular structure topped by a massive cupola. Built in 1884, it was expanded in 1891 with two large wings to make room for Seattle's growing population, and it eventually took up the entire block between 5th and 6th and Battery and Wall. But then during the fourth regrade in 1910, workers lopped off the west wing because it straddled the official regrade boundary.

For the next twenty years, Denny School hovered on the edge of a 40-foot precipice. (For comparison, the brick Devonshire apartment building

REGRADES: THE BUREAUCRACY

Each regrade followed a similar process. When more than 50 percent of the residents who lived in the impacted area signed a petition in favor of the regrade, they presented it to the city council. The council then had to pass an ordinance in support of the project. Finally, a committee appointed by the council examined each property to determine the assessment that each resident would have to pay to the city to regrade the hill. This could vary widely depending upon location, property size, and the value of a person's house. Residents also had to pay the contractor to lower their property, as the city was only responsible for the roads and infrastructure.

on the northwest corner of Wall and 5th Ave is four stories or about 40 feet high.) The city destroyed the rest of Denny School in 1930 when workers completed the final regrade and lowered the hill to its present elevation.

Continue west on Wall Street to 3rd Avenue.

❽ The altered historic building on the northwest corner is the Trianon Building, one of Seattle's most famous dance halls. Opened in May 1927, the Trianon Ballroom could hold 5,000 dancers with seating for an additional 800. It was a great place to see performers such as Guy Lombardo, Duke Ellington, Lionel Hampton, and a teenage Quincy Jones (in 1951, as trumpeter for Hampton's band)—that is, if you were white. The Trianon did not allow African Americans on the dance floor until 1940 and then only on Monday during segregated shows. The ballroom closed in 1956 and morphed into a wrestling arena and later into a retail space before its present manifestation as retail and office space.

Continue west on Wall Street to 2nd Avenue, turn left, or south, and walk down the west side of 2nd to Battery Street.

❾ In addition to the automobile industry, the other large-scale business to move into the post-regrade Denny Hill landscape was also unexpected. For several decades, Seattle was a regional center for the film distribution trade through what were known as film exchanges. Movie-theater owners from Montana, Alaska, Idaho, and Washington came to inspect and rent films sent out by the studios. The first exchange opened in 1909, and within

WASHING AWAY A HILL

Water was the key ingredient for most of Seattle's regrades. For example, the fourth Denny regrade required 23 million gallons of water a day, which came from Elliott Bay and Lake Union. The water traveled from the source through pipes to distribution points on Battery Street. Pumps then fed the water into smaller pipes and out through hydraulic giants, or water cannons, technology that had been developed and perfected in the California Gold Rush. They consisted of a huge water hose with a 7- to 10-foot-long nozzle and an adjustable opening from 3 to 5 inches in diameter. An early article described the water as shooting "into the hillside at a cannon ball rate." The entire contraption sat on an articulated base and could be operated by one person, who aimed the water at the soft sediments of the hill. For locations with more compacted material, workers used dynamite and steam shovels to break up the harder sediments. Flumes then carried the water and washed-away debris out into Elliott Bay.

6 years, 20 operated in downtown. Eventually all of the major studios had exchanges, each with salesmen and often with a screening room. Because the movies were made of highly flammable nitrocellulose film, the buildings were typically made of fireproof concrete with special vaults.

By the end of the 1920s, most of the film exchanges centered on the area around 2nd Avenue and Battery Street, with Columbia, Warner Brothers, Paramount, Universal Studios, and others sharing two massive buildings. Nearby were smaller distribution buildings, including one of the few to survive. In 1936, MGM built the Art Deco–style, black-and-tan, brick- and terra-cotta–clad building on the southwest corner of 2nd and Battery. Basically a warehouse, it had a sales area in the front, a poster room in the middle, and restrooms, an examination room, and six vaults in the rear of the building. MGM used the building until 1960. With the advent of safer film and better distribution networks, the era of the film exchange ended; the last one closed in 1980.

Continue south on 2nd Avenue for one block. About two or three buildings south of Bell Street, look across 2nd to the tallest building: its dormers rise just behind the one-story buildings on the street.

Denny Regrade, May 1910, Asahel Curtis

⑩ The Belltown Funky Studios (2224 2nd Avenue) is the lone pre-regrade structure that has survived. Although many houses were moved off the hill, and a few lowered to the post-regrade elevation, they slowly disappeared as development led to the building of larger structures, particularly in recent decades as Belltown has become more popular. Only the Belltown Funky remains, saved by a recent landmark designation by the city.

Early Seattle real-estate speculator Lewis Rowe built the original structure around 1890, one of 200 apartment buildings added to the city as the population exploded following Seattle's Great Fire of 1889. Rowe's building illustrates the changing fortunes of the regraded landscape. When he built the apartments, which were more elaborate in the early years, the land was assessed at $5,000. By 1905, the value of the land had dropped to $1,750, but when it sold five years later, the assessment had increased to $9,900. Perhaps the additional value induced the new owners to make a radical change. In 1912, they excavated the land the building stood on and built the three-space storefront that still is on the property. Rowe's gabled building became known as the Wayne Apartments, a name that stuck for decades. The land value slipped, however, and by 1942, it was valued at $2,680.

Return north to Bell Street, cross to the north side, and turn right, or east. Walk one block to 3rd. Look south.

⑪ You are standing a bit west of where one of Seattle's most famous photographs was taken—Asahel Curtis's 1910 picture of the high mounds created during the 1908 to 1911 regrade of Denny Hill. To give you an idea of the size of the mounds, look at the Cornelius Building. It is nine stories high or about 110 feet tall, more or less the height of the mound in the foreground, which was coincidentally located just north of where the Cornelius now rises. The mounds were gone by early 1911.

Continue east on Bell Street another block to 4th Avenue, turn right, or south, and walk one block to Blanchard Street.

⑫ You are standing directly below Denny Hill's former northern high point. During the 1908 to 1911 regrade, contractor Grant Smith and Co. and Stillwell washed away 107 feet of sediment, lowering the hill to its present elevation. The total amount of material removed during the regrade would fill about 1,700 Olympic-size swimming pools. Before the regrade, slopes down from the high point ranged between 7 and 22 percent. (With a 19 percent grade, Madison Street between 3rd and 4th Avenues is the steepest downtown street. Other streets in the city are even steeper.)

Walk south on 4th Avenue to Virginia Street, turn right, or west, and walk to 2nd Avenue.

⑬ Look in any direction from this corner, and you will notice a peculiar topographic feature: the four streets descend from where you stand. Congratulations—you have reached the modern high point of Denny Hill's regraded landscape, 167 feet above sea level. This subtle summit exists because of James Moore. From 1903 to 1906 during the regrade of 2nd Avenue, which also included work on side streets, Moore successfully blocked the lowering of 2nd at Virginia Street as planned by R. H. Thomson. The reason: It would increase the cost of transporting goods up Virginia to Moore's Washington Hotel on 3rd. If 2nd had been lowered to Thomson's specifications, Virginia would have been steeper from 2nd to 3rd because 3rd remained at the same elevation. A steeper road would have translated to higher transportation costs due to the additional animals needed to pull wagons up a steeper incline.

Moore's victory mound is the token geographic reminder of the great hill that once stood north of downtown. For most of the city's early history, Denny Hill troubled Seattleites. Although Denny was one of the city's fabled seven hills, which gave Seattle a Romanesque air of distinction, it didn't impress engineers who saw the hill as an impediment to improving transportation within the city. And it may have been a fine place to live with good views, a cherished school, and the city's first park, but Denny also blocked the steady northward advancement of downtown businesses.

Other hills—Beacon and Queen Anne—were also threatened with regrading, but they survived: they were higher and larger. Denny was Seattle's Goldilocks hill. It was big enough to be annoying and yet not too big to scare away the city's ambitious planners. And so, in contrast to the city's other hills, which retained their homes, schools, shops, and churches, Denny was destroyed. A neighborhood and its community were washed off the map, leaving behind a blank slate that only in recent decades has once again become a residential neighborhood.

Walk south on 2nd Avenue to Pine Street, where you began the walk.

Stories in Stone

DOWNTOWN ROCKS

Enjoy a showcase of stone from around the world ranging in age from 80,000 to 3.5 billion years old.

DISTANCE	1.3 miles
START/END	1st Avenue and Madison Street
NOTES	Several buildings on this walk have geologically rich lobbies that are accessible only on weekdays. The walk does not focus on those lobbies but does mention them.

Every time you walk through downtown Seattle, you are walking along a geologic timeline as you pass by buildings made of stone ranging in age from thousands to millions to billions of years old. And that stone is equal to any assembled by plate tectonics. Slate, granite, sandstone, marble, gneiss, and limestone all grace these walls. Plus, builders have gone to the expense of cleaning and polishing the stone, making the fossils and minerals stand out in all their beauty.

Seattle is not unique in this. Most cities of any size have buildings covered in a similar wealth of rocks. In recent years, global trade has been promoted as a new economic trend, and yet building stone has been shipped around the world for centuries. When the Romans conquered Egypt, they promptly demonstrated their victory, and conveyed a message

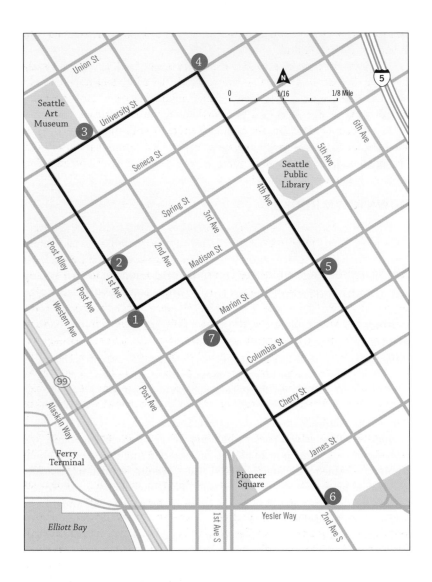

of superiority, by removing granite from Egypt and transporting it back to Rome for use in buildings.

Using stone to express an idea continues today. Look at Seattle's early banks and what do you see? Granite, which their builders hoped would symbolize strength. In contrast, many building lobbies and corporate boardrooms have marble walls—a shorthand for success and elegance.

As philosopher Will Durant famously wrote, "Civilization exists by geologic consent." One of the finer ways to experience Durant's philosophy is through building stone, which not only provides a hands-on introduction to geology but also to human history.

Start on the southwest corner of 1st Avenue and Madison Street.

❶ The story of stone in Seattle began at this corner on June 6, 1889. John E. Back was heating glue in Clairmont and Company's cabinetry shop when his pot of glue boiled over and onto the stove. Back, whom the *Seattle P-I* described as "a thick-set blond of mediocre intelligence," responded eagerly but incorrectly and tossed water on the pot, which exploded the hot glue onto wood shavings on the floor. Soon the entire wooden structure was burning, and within hours, Seattle's Great Fire had torched more than 115 acres and destroyed the downtown retail and industrial core, leaving behind what Rudyard Kipling, who passed through town a few weeks after the fire en route to Vancouver, B.C., called "a horrible black smudge, as though a Hand had come down and rubbed the place smooth." Kipling, then 23 years old and on the verge of fame, added, "I know now what being wiped out means."

The burning of Seattle was a fabulous event for a geo-geek like me, for within days the upstart, proud town vowed to rebuild, but this time with materials that could better withstand fire—rock and brick. Seattle, however, lacks good stone at the surface, so builders sought out the closest quarries, which they found in Index (granite), about 30 miles east of Everett; in Tenino (sandstone), 12 miles southeast of Olympia; in Wilkeson (sandstone), 15 miles east of Tacoma; and at Chuckanut (sandstone) on Bellingham Bay. Not only did the quarries provide good stone, they were also close to good transport networks. The first three were along rail lines, each of which had been established in the 1880s and '90s, whereas Chuckanut stone could be loaded directly onto barges and brought down Puget Sound.

These quarries quickly dominated the Seattle building trade. However, after builders' initial use of the local sandstones and granite, they began to order rock from Vermont and Indiana for variety. Over the subsequent decades as additional money and people flowed into Seattle, building owners desired more exotic material and found it in rocks from as far away as Italy. And finally, as cutting techniques improved and transportation became cheaper, the worldwide stone trade took off and a staggering range of stones were moved across the planet, compelled by the demands of builders. Now you know why rock hounds in Seattle are happy.

Cross 1st Avenue to the east side, and walk one block north to Spring Street. There you will find the Holyoke Building (1022 1st Avenue).

❷ The Holyoke Building was under construction at the time of Seattle's Great Fire, and it was one of the first to be finished after the conflagration. Like many post-fire structures, it uses one of the three local sandstones, in this case the brownish rocks from Chuckanut.

Deposition of the great beds of local sandstone occurred 50 million years ago when the area that would become western Washington lacked the dramatic topography that now dominates. Neither the Cascade Mountains nor the Olympic Mountains existed, and what we think of as the Interstate 5 corridor was oceanfront property. To the east, rivers flowed out of mountains along the Washington-Idaho border and across a broad plain. As the rivers spread toward the ocean, they deposited bed upon bed of sand, which eventually turned into sandstone, one of the most common building materials.

Sandstone can be cut into massive blocks, which work well for building foundations. (Not until the 1904 construction of the Alaska Building did Seattle get a tower with a steel infrastructure.) Sandstone also resists erosion, as can be seen in the well-preserved details of the Holyoke's carved capitals. But sandstone does have a significant drawback. To see it, walk around to the north side of the Holyoke and look at the window sills.

Geologists refer to such broken layers as *spalling*. It occurs because water penetrates the beds and deposits salt crystals, which slowly grow and wedge apart the sandstone layers. Further damage can occur during the infrequent Seattle winters when the temperature drops below freezing and ice forms. When water freezes, it expands about nine percent and has the same damaging effect on sandstone as salt crystals.

Building technique also plays a key role in where and how stone weathers. Ledges are the most common place for building stones to weaken because they are not protected by other rocks. Stacked blocks generally resist weathering better, but salt and ice can also degrade them. If a builder stacks sandstone blocks with their beds vertical and parallel to the building's surface, like an upright book with its cover face out on a book shelf, then these agents of erosion can weaken the stone so that beds peel off one layer at a time. (Please do not test this weathering phenomenon by peeling up a layer yourself.) If the beds lie horizontally, like a book flat on a shelf, water does not easily penetrate the layers and the rock deteriorates more slowly.

Sandstone retained its popularity as a building material in Seattle through the 1920s, but by the end of the Depression, few local quarries produced stone. At present, only the Wilkeson and Tenino quarries remain open, mostly supplying small quantities of rock for restoration work.

Walk two blocks north along 1st Avenue to University Street. Turn right on University and continue one block to the northwest corner of 2nd Avenue.

❺ This corner provides an opportunity to see one of the most beautiful uses of brick—the other great building material that became popular after 1889. This fine example of brick is in the Seattle Tower (1218 3rd Avenue), one block east at the southeast corner of 3rd Avenue and University. Originally known as the Northern Life Tower (1929), it got its new name when it was sold in 1967.

Designed by Abraham Albertson, Joseph Wilson, and Paul Richardson for Northern Life Insurance, the building was inspired by the "enduring and inspiring character of the neighboring Cascades and Olympics," wrote Albertson. He conceived it "as rising out of the ground, not as sitting traditionally upon the surface—as part of the earth rather than a thing apart of it."

To accomplish this and to convey the feeling of a mountain with its dark forested slopes leading up to the lighter, snow-covered summit, the building grades in color from heather brown bricks at the base to light tan at the top. Brick makers produced four main color groups by altering the chemistry (iron ore and manganese) at the kiln. Each day, a "competent man" would select which bricks would achieve the appropriate blend of colors fading from dark at the bottom to light at the top. The white bands of "snow" at the top are terra-cotta, and the three spires on the building's summit represent trees.

In contrast to its lack of stone, Seattle is rich in the ingredients for brick. All brick makers had to do was scoop out the Lawton Clay deposited during the last ice age and fire it into bricks. Many early brick factories opened along the Duwamish River, with larger ones at Renton and in the former town of Taylor, in the Cedar River Watershed. The brick used in the Seattle Tower was made from clay excavated at the base of Beacon Hill, where today's Spokane Street Viaduct intersects Interstate 5.

Walk two blocks east to the northeast corner of 4th Avenue and the oatmeal-colored, hole-filled stone at the base of the Rainier Tower (1301 Fifth Avenue).

❹ Like Rome, Seattle was built on seven hills. Both cities also share a building stone: a type of limestone known as travertine. Coincidentally, most of the travertine used in Seattle buildings came from quarries in Tivoli, about 20 miles east of Rome. These quarries provided stone for the Colosseum and St. Peter's Colonnade in Rome, as well as the Getty Center in Los Angeles, the best known travertine-clad building in this country. All of the rock from the quarries formed less than 200,000 years ago with a peak around 80,000 years ago, making this some of the youngest stone in the building trade.

Unlike the Salem Limestone at the next stop on the walk, travertine does not form in the sea. Instead, it precipitates from calcite-rich water expelled from springs or in caves. A modern example is Yellowstone National Park's Mammoth Hot Springs, where hot water rises through cracks and emerges in pools. When this occurs, the calcite in the water settles and accumulates layer upon layer. It can occur so quickly that a half-inch-thick bed can form in a single year. In contrast, marine-deposited limestone takes thousands of years to deposit a single inch of calcite.

These calcite beds are readily apparent in the Rainier Tower, though each panel is rotated 90 degrees from how the beds originally formed. What you see then is a cross-section of the beds. The pockets, or holes in the rock, developed where calcite accumulated around a foreign body such as a stick or leaf.

Seattle builders used travertine indoors and out. In some structures, like the Washington Federal Savings Building (425 Pike Street), they filled in the holes in the bedding. This is for preventative maintenance. In a colder location, such as Boston, water seeps into the cracks, freezes, expands, and breaks the stone. Seattle's moderate winter climate, however, has little effect on the travertine. Another travertine-clad structure is the IBM Building (1200 5th Avenue). What unites it and the Rainier Tower is their design by Seattle native Minoru Yamasaki, best known as the man who designed the World Trade Towers.

> Walk south on 4th Avenue four blocks and cross Marion Street to the brick Rainier Club (820 4th Avenue). Stop about 50 feet down the block at the second section of retaining wall north of the entrance. The top of the wall should be at a good viewing height.

❺ The cream-colored stone atop the brick walls of the Rainier Club is Salem Limestone, quarried near Bedford, Indiana. It became popular following the 1893 World's Columbian Exposition, when the fair's White City popularized white as *the* color for buildings. As far as I have been able to determine, Salem Limestone is the only stone used in all 50 states, including structures such as the Empire State Building (amazingly, the hole

Fossils in the Salem Limestone

OTHER FOSSILS IN SEATTLE BUILDINGS

Westlake Mall Floor (400 Pine Street): This is made from 175-million-year-old limestone from France. Fossils include solitary corals, which from above resemble a clock face without the numbers and from the side look like an ice cream cone; brachiopods, marine animals often mistaken for clams; and snails.

Grand Hyatt Hotel (721 Pine Street), Food Court Concourse A and B at SeaTac Airport, and Cherry Hill branch of Swedish Hospital (500 17th Avenue): These are made from gray 155-million-year-old limestone quarried in Germany. Fossils include ammonites, which look like a cross section of a cinnamon roll; belemnites, which look like a cigar; and sponges, the darker irregular shapes.

where the stone was quarried still exists as no more stone has come out of it), the Pentagon, and more than 750 post offices. (The Salem also plays a central role in the movie *Breaking Away*.)

Deposition of the Salem occurred 300 to 330 million years ago in a shallow, clear, tropical sea, when what we think of as the American Midwest looked like the Bahamas. The warm waters supported a diverse range of swimming, crawling, and bottom-dwelling invertebrates. When these creatures died, their bodies accumulated in a watery cemetery on the seafloor, eventually solidifying into a 40-to-100-foot-thick stone menagerie. This matrix of corpses formed a limestone that can be cut cleanly and evenly in all directions.

To see some of these fossils, look at the limestone blocks atop the retaining wall. The most common recognizable fossils are one-eighth- to one-third-inch-wide discs of crinoids, a relative of starfish and sand dollars. Crinoids resemble plants with a root-like base, a flexible stem made of stacked discs, and a flower-like body. Another common fossil is from a colonial animal known as a bryozoan, which looks a bit like Rice Chex cereal. Wave action from long-ago tides broke up most of the shells from the animals that plied the ancient sea, but careful investigation also reveals brachiopods, which look like clam shells, and ice-cone shaped corals.

Cross to the west side of 4th Avenue, walk south, to Cherry Street, turn right, or west, and continue two blocks to 2nd Avenue. Turn left at 2nd, and stay on the east side until you reach the Smith Tower (502–508 2nd Avenue) at Yesler Way.

❻ When it opened on July 4, 1914, the 462-foot Smith Tower was the tallest building west of Ohio. Over the years, the mostly terra-cotta–clad edifice has been the victim of many incorrect claims, including being the fourth tallest building in the world, the tallest outside of New York, and Seattle's first skyscraper. Although all of these claims are false, it is a beautiful building well worth visiting.

Most worthy of notice is the Index granite on the exterior. This was the other local rock that was brought into Seattle following the Great Fire. The quarry opened in 1894, just two years after the Great Northern Railroad laid tracks along the Skykomish River. The quarry is now a popular rock-climbing area. In addition to its use in many downtown buildings, the Index granite is found in curbs throughout Seattle (see Curbology in Walk 13 for more detail).

Like most granites, the salt-and-pepper–colored Index rock formed when one tectonic plate collided with another. About 35 million years ago the dense iron- and magnesium-rich oceanic plate known as the Farallon (now called the Juan de Fuca Plate) began diving under, or subducting, the lighter, silica- and aluminum-rich North American Plate. As the Farallon slid deeper, its leading edge started to melt, forming magma, which cooled and solidified into granite deep underground. Note the dark blobs within the Index granite, which geologists call *xenoliths*, or foreign rocks. They are pieces of older rock incorporated into the magma. Quarry workers refer to the blobs as "heathens" because they disrupt the stone's homogenous texture.

The Smith Tower has one of the most dazzling lobbies found in the city. On the walls are beige onyx panels from Baja California. The panel pattern is known as book-matching and is achieved by cutting a block into slices and mirroring the layers. Similar to travertine, the calcite-rich onyx forms in springs but in cold water instead of hot. Color in the onyx comes from minute quantities of iron and manganese. Up the stairs are white and black panels of marble quarried on Marble Island in southeast Alaska. Known as Alaskan or Tokeen marble, it was a widely used building stone in Seattle. (If you have the chance to use a restroom in the Seattle Tower, you will find stunning Alaskan marble panels that are more black than white.)

Walk north four blocks on 2nd Avenue to Marion Street and the Exchange Building (821 2nd Avenue) on the southwest corner.

3.5-billion-year-old Morton Gneiss

❼ I can pretty much guarantee that the black-and-pink rock on the Exchange Building is the oldest rock you will ever see. (If I am wrong, you are mighty lucky.) At 3.524 billion years old, it began to form when Earth was just an adolescent, about 1.1 billion years old. Known to geologists as the Morton Gneiss and to the stone industry as Rainbow Granite, the Exchange Building stone is quarried in Morton, Minnesota, a small town about 100 miles west of the Twin Cities.

Gneiss is a type of metamorphic rock, meaning it started life as one type of rock (in this case a relative of granite) that was squeezed and baked, changing the texture and mineral assemblage. With the Morton, metamorphism occurred when two tectonic plates collided. Marble is also a metamorphic rock, which was limestone before it underwent metamorphosis.

One of the more beautiful building stones in the world, the Morton Gneiss is also worth noticing because of its age. The oldest commonly accepted evidence for life on Earth are fossils of single-celled organisms that lived around 3.5 billion years ago. This means that the Morton began to form when Earth didn't look anything like it does now. No plants, no animals, and without them, fewer colors. So I encourage you to reach out and touch this rock; you will be experiencing one of the most provocative concepts that geologists have contributed to modern thought, what writer John McPhee called "deep time," or the nearly unimaginable spans of millions and billions of years of Earth's history.

The more recent history of Morton Gneiss is also noteworthy. First quarried in the early 1880s, it peaked in popularity in the 1920s and 1930s, particularly in Art Deco architecture. The organic feel of the swirling patterns both complemented and contrasted with Art Deco's geometric designs such as zigzags and chevrons. Designers also used the Morton's bold colors in counterpoint to the light-colored stone often used above buildings' bases and to help draw attention to buildings' entryways.

Before leaving, if you have a chance, go into the Exchange Building's lobby. It is a classic with beautiful book-matched panels of Italian Portoro Limestone, quarried about 15 miles from Carrara, where Michelangelo obtained his marble. Minute amounts of organic material make the limestone black. Subsequent alteration of the stone caused fractures, which filled with calcite, giving the Portoro its complex texture. The stone of the floor is Italian travertine.

In this age of concrete, glass, and titanium, it may seem anachronistic to marvel at building stone. But for centuries, stone was the material of choice, and it is still the preferred material for those wishing to convey classic elegance and beauty in their architecture. Reasonably fireproof, infinitely colored, and readily available, stone has qualities unmatched by any other substance. Knowing that a building's success or failure often rests on the choice of stone, architects and builders continue to comb the globe, from Italian hillsides to Midwestern river valleys, searching for the perfect rock for their structures.

Walk north one block to Madison Street. Turn left to return to this walk's starting point.

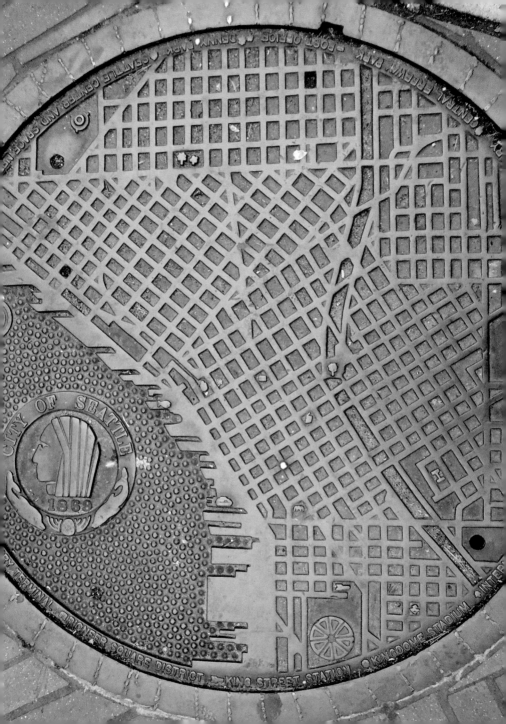

Where You At?

A DOWNTOWN GEOGRAPHICAL TOUR

Wander in and out of buildings to explore
historic maps, clocks, and photographs.

DISTANCE	1.1 miles, one way
STARTING POINT	James Street and Yesler Way
ENDING POINT	Westlake Mall on 4th Avenue between Pike and Pine Streets
NOTES	Because this walk takes you into office buildings, it is best done on a weekday. On weekends, you can still access the Rainier Tower but will not be able to enter the lobby of the Seattle Tower. There is one relatively steep hill near the beginning.

If you ask Seattle residents how to get to a particular spot in the downtown area, you are likely to hear them mutter, "Jesus Christ Made Seattle Under Pressure." No, your interlocutors are not seeking help from on high. As many in Seattle know, this pithy saying is the order of downtown city streets: Jefferson-James, Cherry-Columbia, Marion-Madison, Spring-Seneca, University-Union, and Pike-Pine. But there are other ways of knowing where you are in downtown Seattle. One of my favorites can be found at your feet, on more than a dozen manhole covers—sometimes called hatch covers—each decorated with a map of downtown. Or if you

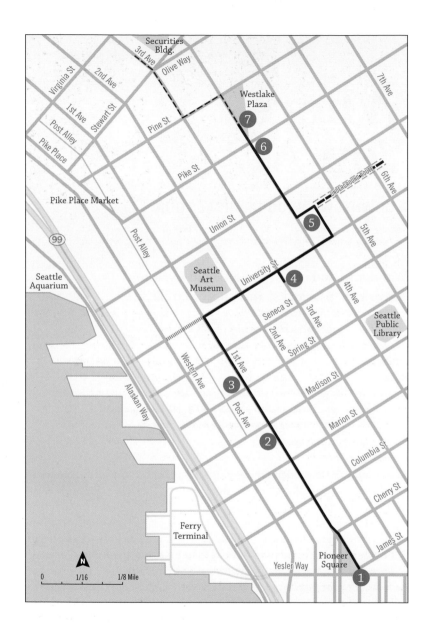

Earl Laymen street clock, built in 1922, originally in front of Young's Jewelry, 3rd Avenue and Seneca Street, and now at 1st Avenue S and S Main Street

Question mark clock, built in 1990 by Bill Whipple, 5th Avenue and Pine Street

Ben Bridge street clock, built in 1925 by Joseph Mayer, 4th Avenue and Pike Street

want a more timely perspective, look for the half dozen early-20th-century street clocks that still loom over the city's sidewalks.

Each of the urban elements featured in this walk offers a clue to a better understanding of Seattle's story. They reveal how the city has grown, how it has recovered from catastrophe, and how its citizens see themselves in relation to the larger world. Most are helpful, some are fanciful, and others are occasionally misleading. Made of brass and stone and steel, they provide a sense of permanence, which contrasts sharply to the rapidly changing urban infrastructure. They even offer you a chance to test your knowledge of Seattle history via a series of questions.

Start on the north side of the intersection of James Street and Yesler Way at the corner of the Pioneer Building (600 1st Avenue). Carved into the building on the left side of the steps behind an iron balustrade are the words *City Datum Elev. 18.79.*

❶ Seattle's history began on November 13, 1851, when the *Exact* dropped off 22 members of what became known as the Denny Party at Alki Point in West Seattle. They quickly realized the location was ill suited for building a port, so they moved across Elliott Bay to a spot about 100 yards west of where this walk begins. From this location, the town grew with businesses centered around what is now Pioneer Square and residences on the slopes that rose from the bay.

Although one of the founding fathers, Arthur Denny, was a surveyor, more than two decades passed before the young town had a systematic, accurate, and block-by-block survey. Before this survey, property owners established their property boundaries and fence lines in a haphazard way, often based on their neighbor's previous, unguided planning. For example, at one location a fence that should have been on a property line was actually located nine feet into the street. Finally, in 1875, the city council hired an engineering firm to lay out an accurate grid of the city and note elevations above sea level.

The survey team's first task was to ascertain what is known as the city's *datum point*, or the zero point from which all vertical measurements are made. Engineers and surveyors would use the datum point primarily for establishing new grades on city streets. In addition, with an accurate map based on the datum point, property owners would be able to build structures at an elevation corresponding to the prescribed grade.

To determine the datum point, the surveyors set up a tide gauge on one of the downtown wharves, measured tides over the month of June, and used the mean of the high tides as zero elevation, or in this case, sea level. Next, they transferred the elevation information to a permanent location where later surveyors could easily find it. At the time, one of the few granite buildings in the city was the Dexter Horton Bank, located at what is now the corner of S Washington Street and 1st Avenue S. Unfortunately, Mr. Horton's bank was ruined in Seattle's Great Fire of 1889, which led the City Council to have a new datum point established. On September 16, 1891, it designated that spot as the "lower step at the entrance to the Pioneer block . . . at the southwest corner thereof," or the location where you now stand.

So what does that number carved in granite mean? It means that you are standing 18.79 feet above sea level, or the zero elevation point—or at least this was true until 2003. Because the old datum was based on "inconsistent and outdated methods," the City Council passed an ordinance to establish a new vertical reference datum. Subsequent advances in technology, using tools such as the Global Positioning System, have led to further changes, which means that surveyors no longer rely upon a single point to establish their location.

Walk north on the west side of 1st Avenue, cross Marion Street, and continue to slightly beyond the entrance of the brick and terra-cotta Federal Building (909 1st). Look for a light pole next to the street. On it are polished metal panels inscribed with newspaper articles from 1889.

❷ Artists Linda Beaumont, Stuart Keeler, and Michael Machnic made this artwork titled *The Fire* in 1996 as an homage to Seattle's Great Fire of June 6, 1889. (For more information about the fire, see Walk 3.) On the map just below the title panel, look very carefully for a star at Madison Street and Front Street (now 1st Avenue). It marks where the fire started. The map also illustrates how much Seattle's shoreline has changed; all of the docks and wharfs from 1889 would now be on land made by fill.

Walk north on 1st Avenue, and cross to the northwest corner of Spring Street.

❸ Look down at the manhole cover at your feet and its map of Seattle. Designer Anne Knight thought that the map would make an excellent teaching guide, as well as a route finder to downtown. Around the map's outer edge, she added a key to the symbols used for different Seattle landmarks. Look for a raised, polished bead, which indicates the location of the manhole cover on the map. All of the landmarks still exist except for the Kingdome, Seattle's former sports arena, which was imploded on March 26, 2000. Knight told me, "At the time when I designed these maps the

Hatch cover by Nathan Jackson, 1976   Hatch cover by Garth Edwards, 1984

Kingdome had just been built, and I thought naively that it looked like a structure that would be there forever."

Nineteen covers were planned. Only 14 can still be seen; one supposedly went to Kobe, Japan, as part of a sister city project, while others simply disappeared or were never made. Each cost $200 and weighed 230 pounds. The first one was put in place in April 1977 on the north edge of Occidental Park. It is still there.

Seattle Arts Commissioner Jacquetta Blanchett Freeman started the city's manhole cover program. She had been inspired by decorated covers she had seen in Florence, Italy. Working with the Department of Community Development director, Paul Schell, she raised the money to hire Knight for the first design. More recent manhole covers include artwork by Garth Edwards (1984), Nathan Jackson (1976), and Nancy Blum (2001).

Also, note the duck tracks a few feet west of Knight's cover.

Continue north on 1st Avenue to University Street, turn right, or east, and walk two blocks to 3rd Avenue. Cross over to the entrance to the Seattle Tower (1218 3rd). Enter the lobby if it is open. If not, simply admire the beauty of the building.

❹ As described in Stories in Stone (Walk 3), the Seattle Tower is supposed to represent a mountain. To complement the mountain symbolism, "the lobby was first conceived as a tunnel carved out of the solid, the side walls polished, the floor worn smooth and the ceiling incised and decorated as a civilized caveman might do it," wrote architect Abraham Albertson. Apparently, said caveman also had quite the knowledge of the world, for at the end of the lobby is a bronze-colored plaster bas-relief map of the world, titled "Westward the Course of Empire Takes Its Way." The title comes from Bishop George Berkeley's poem *America or the Muse's Refuge: A Prophecy*, written in 1726 and one of the most famous evocations of America's destined greatness.

Perhaps the map should have been titled "Seattle, Where the Course of Empire Leads." No means of transportation on land or sea illustrated on the map is more advanced than the great ship leaving Seattle and the fast-moving train headed our way. Nor is any building on the map larger than the one in Seattle, which of course just happens to be the one you are standing in. Like the building itself, the map is a brilliant piece of symbolic propaganda for a city on the rise.

"Westward the Course of Empire Takes Its Way," Seattle Tower lobby

It is not known who designed the map, but Joseph Wilson's daughter, Mary Basetti, told me, "I always felt that [the map] was Dad's doing because the design well captures his unique drawing style. Dad loved everything about the Northwest, and I would think he was expressing our special location as an important port city."

Exit the lobby. Walk east on University to 4th Avenue, cross to the north side of the street, and continue on University one half block to the entrance of the Rainier Tower. Enter the building, walk down the stairs and through the lobby to a corridor, or pedestrian concourse. Turn right, and walk down the lengthy corridor to see an excellent display of photographs of Seattle. The corridor ends at an escalator.

❺ These photographs focus on the Klondike Gold Rush, Maritime Seattle, Boeing, and Seattle's growth. There is also a large terra-cotta head of a Native American, which came from the White-Henry-Stuart Block, the building leveled in 1978 for the Rainier Tower. Other heads from that building ended up at the Washington State Convention Center and Discovery Park. The Cobb Building across the street still retains its original heads, including one in the vestibule adjacent to the entrance.

Where the Rainier Tower now stands is part of the Metropolitan Tract, the location of the original University of Washington campus. In 1861, early Seattle settlers Arthur and Mary Denny, Charles and Mary Terry, and Edward Lander donated 10 acres for a university site. Classes began on November 4, 1861, in a building later replaced by today's Fairmont Olympic Hotel. The campus moved to its present location in 1895 to be "removed from the excitements and temptations incident to city life and its environment," or so noted an annual report from the university. UW still owns the tract, which has about 1.7 million square feet of office space and annually generates more than $20 million in net income.

> Return to the beginning of the corridor, turn right, descend the stairs to the building's main lobby. Turn left and exit to 4th Avenue. Turn right, and walk north to the southeast corner of 4th and Pike Street and the street clock in front of Ben Bridge Jewelers.

6 In this era when everyone carries a phone that displays the time, it may seem strange that people used to rely on sidewalk street clocks for their chronometric updates. So many horological devices once graced downtown that Seattle was known as the "city of clocks." It was also home to one of the great clock makers, Joseph Mayer, who began working with his brother in 1897 and continued making cast-iron street clocks until 1937. Clock aficionados have located surviving Mayer clocks as far away as Puerto Rico and New York.

At 4th and Pike in 1930, one could see 16 clocks from the corner. Most had been erected by jewelers, which led to a clock war as each jeweler tried to outdo the other, first with two dials, then four, then eight. Never had telling time been so easy in Seattle, though there was still some confusion, as "it is seldom that any two of the clocks show the same time," noted a writer in the *Seattle Times* in 1930.

Seattle's golden age of clocks, when 50 graced the streets, did not last long. In 1953, the Board of Public Works proposed to eliminate street clocks, noting their "obsolescence and homeliness" and complaining that they often displayed the wrong time and sometimes several incorrect times on clocks with multiple dials. The Board ultimately decided to allow the clocks to remain but only if clock owners ensured their accuracy. Otherwise the clocks could be removed or have a cloak placed over them.

In 1980, the city of Seattle designated as landmarks 10 of the old street clocks. Nine of the landmarked ones still exist, including three in downtown. Built by Joseph Mayer in 1925, the Ben Bridge clock is the only one in

Seattle's forest of clocks, as seen looking east on 4th Avenue, June 1930

Seattle that has remained in the family of its original owners. Still with its original timing mechanism, it has to be wound once a week.

Cross Pike Street, and walk north into Westlake Plaza.

❼ Artist Robert Maki and landscape architect Robert Hanna patterned the gray, white, and red granite paving blocks after a Salish basket motif. Maki also incorporated large reddish granite pieces to evoke the original seven hills that Seattle was built on. Less obvious, and a little challenging to find, are numerous bronze panels placed among the paving blocks. (The twenty-plus panels are located about halfway between Maki's northern-

OPTIONAL SIDE TRIP: AN OLD WEATHER GAUGE

Completed in 1913, the Securities Building, which takes up the northeast corner of 3rd Avenue and Stewart Street, has a beautiful and unusual lobby. It features white banded onyx quarried in Baja California. The stone formed in cold water springs as calcite settled out of the water and built up layer upon layer. Building-stone onyx is sometimes called onyx marble or Mexican onyx, though it is not marble and not all of it comes from Mexico [the same rock is used in the lobby of the Smith Tower (Walk 3)]. The green rock is serpentine, a metamorphic rock (meaning it was altered by pressure and temperature) quarried in Vermont and known as Verde Antique.

Equally as intriguing and far more unusual is the Weather Center and its six gauges. Building tenant Time Outdoor, Inc., which was a subsidiary of the weather station builder American Sign and Indicators Corporation, installed the display in 1964. It had hoped to promote the product, but apparently it met with little success as no other building in Seattle added its own Weather Center. The Securities Building's time, wind direction, and barometric gauges work; the others have been broken for years, and the property owner has not been able to find anyone who can fix them.

most pink granite feature and the waterfall feature, roughly across from the entrance of 1525, 4th on the west side of the street. They may be hidden by tables and chairs, so finding them can be challenging.)

Based on geographic and historic questions and answers created by local children, the panels are oriented in three rows each consisting of four question tiles and one answer tile. In addition, look for a bronze compass a few feet south of the Q&A tiles. Nearby are artistic depictions of several Seattle landmarks, including the Space Needle, Ferry Terminal, Husky Stadium, and the Kingdome. Note how each one is in the correct geographic orientation, creating a rough map of the Seattle landscape.

With smart phones and GPS, knowing your time, temperature, and place in the world has never been easier, but sometimes it's nice not to rely on technology. Fortunately, you can still find yourself in Seattle.

Star Axis/Seven Hills by Robert Maki and Robert Hanna

Who's Watching You?

A DOWNTOWN MENAGERIE
IN STONE AND TERRA-COTTA

This urban safari showcases the many
animals that adorn downtown buildings.

DISTANCE	1.8 miles, one way
STARTING POINT	Western Avenue and Blanchard Street
ENDING POINT	Columbia Street between 2nd and 3rd Avenues
NOTES	A pair of binoculars will enhance your viewing of some of the features on this walk. An optional side trip adds three-quarters of a mile.

Do you ever have the feeling that you are being watched when you stroll through downtown Seattle? You are probably right. Hundreds of eyes peer out from buildings tracking your actions. These observers are neither human nor electronic. Instead, a bestiary of animals watches you. A tour of the urban core reveals a veritable Noah's Ark's worth of carved and molded beasts stalking your every step.

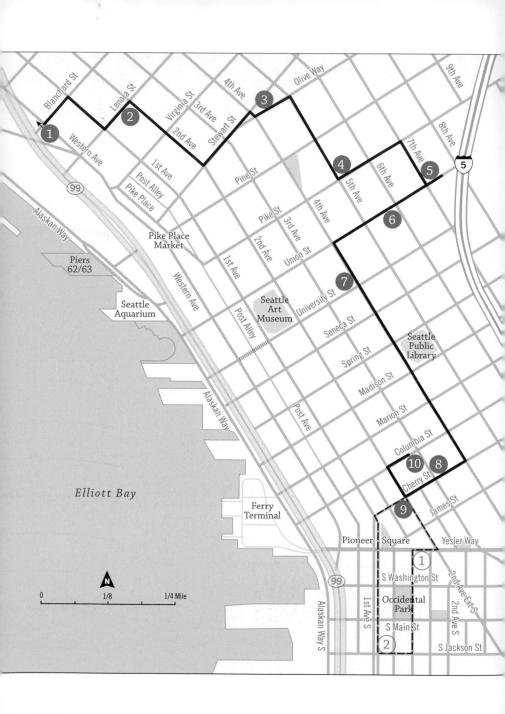

Animal and human ornamentation peaked between 1890 and 1940 in the heyday of terra-cotta cladding in Seattle. Terra-cotta is a kind of brick made by pressing moist clay into a plaster mold. After firing, a glaze is applied, which can be any color or texture. Architects turned to terra-cotta following Seattle's Great Fire of 1889 because it is fireproof and lighter than stone. In addition, molded terra-cotta can be mass produced easily and more cheaply than carving the same feature out of stone. The main producers were local businesses, including Northern Clay Company and Denny-Renton Clay and Coal Company, and two from out of state, Northwestern Terra Cotta and Gladding, McBean, and Company.

Terra-cotta is not the only medium used in downtown animals and figures; many are formed from stone. Part of what makes these carvings enchanting is that they have weathered over time, and formerly crisp features have changed and given the faces more character.

This walk passes by lions, eagles, dolphins, walruses, and a duck, as well as a few rather odd looking humans. Some are well known, but many are seldom noticed and a few can best be appreciated with binoculars. Just like going on a Serengeti safari, you will need good instincts and stout shoes, though you may also want an ORCA pass and a coffee mug.

Start on the northwest corner of Western Avenue and Blanchard Street, across the street from the Union Stables Building (2200 Western Avenue).

Union Stables Building

❶ Walk down any street of stores, and you will find symbolic clues to what happens (or happened) behind the facades. Perhaps it's a neon cocktail glass for a tavern, granite columns for a bank, or a giant cross for a church. In 1910, when the Union Stables opened, probably the simplest way to figure out what happened in the building was the scent of horses, but failing that, a passerby's quick glance at the top of the brick structure would reveal a horse head, a sure sign of an equine line of business.

Union Stables is one of the few remaining buildings from the era when actual horses provided much of the horsepower in Seattle. Horses pulled street trolleys, fire engines, carts, and wagons for businesses and individuals. According to Polk's Seattle City Directory, at least 17 public livery, sale, and boarding stables dotted the urban landscape in 1890, with a peak of 37 in 1910. Western Avenue was one of the equine centers with 7 livery stables located on the street in 1905. With the rise of the automobile as the primary means of transportation, however, only 3 stables remained in the city by 1928.

As horses became less important to everyday life, the Union Stables Building took on a new life. On December 18, 1923, the Seattle police confiscated more than $25,000 worth of high-grade booze in "one of the biggest liquor raids" in Seattle during Prohibition. Acting on a mysterious tip, policemen pounded down a heavily padlocked door in the back of the stables and found a room packed floor to ceiling with 230 cases of liquor. Most were labeled with the addresses of prominent Seattle citizens. In 2015, adaptive reuse preserved the Union Stables' structural interiors, which are now used for office space.

Walk east on Blanchard one block to 1st Avenue, turn right, and walk one block to Lenora Street. Turn left, and walk up the south side of Lenora to 2nd Avenue. Note the terra-cotta on the Cristalla Condominium Building (2033 2nd Avenue) on the southwest corner.

❷ One look at the terra-cotta motifs on the former Crystal Pool Natatorium, and you should know what once went on within this building. Covering the walls are mermaids, gaping dolphins, shells, and fantastic fish, along with a chimera-like beast sporting wings, a lion's head, and a fish tail. In 1914, B. Marcus Priteca designed the natatorium, which featured a 260,000-gallon saltwater pool and stands for 1,500 spectators. Each day, pumps brought a new supply of water from Elliott Bay and sent it through filters to massive boilers that heated the water. Crystal Pool quickly became a popular destination for Seattleites.

The building could also be turned into a venue for boxing matches by draining the pool, covering it, and erecting a ring. Bouts were held regularly through the 1930s. By the end of the decade, fewer and fewer people were using the natatorium, and in 1943, the Bethel Temple purchased the property and converted the pool area to a sanctuary. Bethel stayed until

Times Square Building

1999. The new building, the Cristalla, went up in 2003, within the shell of the former natatorium.

> Walk two blocks south on 2nd Avenue to Stewart Street. Turn left, and walk east two blocks to the east side of 4th Avenue. Turn right, and cross to the south side of Olive Way. Turn left, and walk down Olive about half a block until you are directly across the street from the entrance to the triangle-shaped Times Square Building (414 Olive).

❸ Animals also appear on buildings to project a symbolic trait, as exemplified by the Times Square Building. Constructed in 1915, when five daily papers provided the news of the fast-growing metropolis, the goal of the new building was to highlight the importance of the *Seattle Times,* the city's largest daily paper. Not only did the architects, Bebb & Gould, design the paper's headquarters to tower over the nearby structures, they also embellished it with two of the most classic symbols of power—nobility and authority. Look up to find 18 eagles and the heads of 61 lions. Clearly, passersby should think that the *Seattle Times* of the early 20th century was both a force to be reckoned with and one imbued with great American values.

And in case anyone didn't know what the *Times* did, above the main entrance on Olive Way is a terra-cotta triptych illustrating newspaper production. On the left, two allegorical figures gather the news of the world via an elaborate wire network. The central panel illustrates a newspaper office with printer, linotype operator, and pressman. On the right is a newsboy carrying his papers flanked by a man and woman reading the finished product.

The *Times* remained at this location from 1916 until 1932. The building name derived in part from its wedge-shaped resemblance to the *New York Times*'s headquarters, which rose above the Big Apple's Times Square.

Continue east on Olive Way to 5th Avenue, turn right, or south, and walk two blocks on 5th Avenue to Pike Street and Banana Republic (500 Pike Street).

❹ Now the site of a Banana Republic store, this terra-cotta clad structure started as one of the world's first grand movie palaces. When the Coliseum Theater (whose name is emblazoned high on the building on both 5th and Pike) opened on January 8, 1916, general admission was 15 cents with reserved loge seating going for 50 cents. An advertisement in the *Seattle Times* lured patrons with a 2,149-pipe organ, 2,400 extra-wide seats, and air that was "pre-heated and moistened in winter or ice cooled in summer."

Natatorium architect B. Marcus Priteca designed the Coliseum. Best known as a theater architect, Priteca did work with the Pantages theater chain from California to Canada. His other Seattle projects included the Admiral Theater (West Seattle), Congregation Bikur Cholim (now Langston Hughes Cultural Center), and Longacres Racetrack (demolished).

As Priteca did with the natatorium and many of his theaters, he combined a wealth of classical details, from urns to acanthus leaves to oxen heads, 47 of which stare out from the facade. The use of these skulls, known as *bucranium*, has a long history as an architectural feature. An early way to appease Roman and Greek gods had been to sacrifice animals, lop off their heads, decorate them with garlands of fruit and flowers, and hang the heads from the gods' temples. Eventually, the real sacrifice gave way to the allusive motif.

In 1990, the Coliseum closed, a victim of the expansion of the multiplex theater. Two years later, Banana Republic signed a long-term lease and renovated the building, which opened in 1994. Although closed to the public, the building's original balcony still exists.

> Walk east two blocks on Pike to 7th Avenue. Turn right on 7th, walk one block south to Union Street, and turn left to the entrance of ACT Theater (700 Union Street).

❺ Eagles were another commonly used symbol of strength, courage, and dignity, as can be seen on what was originally Aerie No. 1 for the Fraternal Order of Eagles. It is now known as Kreielsheimer Place, home to A Contemporary Theatre (ACT). The Eagles organization started in Seattle when a group of theater managers got together in 1898 and formed the "Seattle Order of Good Things." Two years later, they became the FOE, with the goals of "promoting peace, prosperity, gladness, and hope." Apparently a picture of an eagle on a wall led to the new name.

Designed by Henry Bittman and Harold Adams and completed in 1925, the building features more than 20 eagles on the exterior. The largest of the eagles, in the tympanum above the main door on Union Street, was an "unprecedented achievement" according to a City of Seattle Landmarks Designation report. The terra-cotta bird was cast in a single piece at a cost of $2,100. Additional eagles inside the building grace paintings and door fixtures.

Aerie No. 1 originally contained 81 apartments, a lounge, a library, parlors for members' wives, and an auditorium that could seat 4,000. In the 1960s, performers included the Doors, Jimi Hendrix, and the Grateful Dead. Martin Luther King Jr. also spoke here in November 1961 during his only visit to Seattle. Along with the Paramount Theater, the Eagles Building was saved from destruction by concerns voiced by the arts organization Allied Arts and aided by a $3 million pledge from the Seattle City Council, which led to ACT moving in and renovating the structure.

> Walk one block west on Union to 6th Avenue and the Washington Athletic Club (WAC; 1325 6th Avenue).

❻ For another example of eagles and ones on a much higher perch, look up to the top of the WAC, where massive birds wrap around the corners.

Washington Athletic Club

Cobb Building

Binoculars also reveal stylized human and animal masks running in horizontal rows on several floors of the building. Architect Sherwood Ford designed the building, like many others constructed in the late 1920s and early 1930s, in the Art Deco style, with a stepped-back tower, geometric designs, and stylized motifs.

Walk two blocks west to 4th Avenue, cross over to the west side of 4th, and turn left, or south. Walk most of the block to the Cobb Building (1301 4th Avenue). On the right is an alcove with a large terra-cotta head.

❼ The Cobb Building was the first on the West Coast devoted exclusively to doctors and dentists. With its feather headdress, the head in this alcove is clearly not based on local Native Americans, though it was made by a local craftsman, Victor Schneider, who worked at the Denny-Renton Clay and Coal Company. (He also created the terra-cotta triptych on the *Seattle Times* Building.) The architects who designed the Cobb were the New York firm of Howells and Stokes, who also incorporated the same heads into the White-Henry-Stuart Block, which was destroyed to make way for the Rainier Tower across the street. To see additional heads at the top of the Cobb, cross to the east side of 4th.

The next section of the walk covers several blocks with no stops. Enjoy the interesting buildings, and keep your eyes open for details, such as the manhole cover on the northwest corner of 4th and Marion; it's a map of Seattle.

HOW TO REFURBISH A WALRUS HEAD!

Step 1: Decapitate an original head and ship it to New York. Only a handful of companies in the US are capable of high-volume terra-cotta production. Contractors on the Arctic Building renovation worked with Boston Valley, based in Orchard Park, NY.

Step 2: Produce high-quality drawings of the head.

Step 3: Hand-sculpt a mold eight percent larger than necessary to allow shrinkage as it dries. The mold consists of four or five pieces, which are assembled to create the head.

Step 4. Hand press clay into mold. The head is hollow and lightweight. The tusks are solid and bolted onto the head. Each mold can make between five and ten pieces.

Step 5: Let dry for a week. Hand glaze. Fire for five days.

"This process is essentially the same as it was 100 years ago," said an employee at Boston Valley.

Total Cost: $6,000 to $7,000 for the first head; after the mold is made, $550 for each additional head.

Walk south on 4th to Cherry Street, turn right, or west, and walk down the north side of Cherry to the marble stairway at the former Arctic Club of Seattle Building—now a DoubleTree by Hilton (700 3rd Avenue)

➑ Look up to see what are arguably the best-known animals in Seattle: the 27 walrus heads that adorn the Arctic Building. Designed by Augustus Warren Guild and opened in 1917, the building formerly housed the Arctic Club, a social gathering place for those who wanted to promote Alaska and its resources and perhaps to bandy about tales of the north. It became a hotel in 2008.

As so often happens with infamous beasts, the walruses are obscured by murky layers of misinformation. Rumor one: The tusks were made of ivory or marble. The reality: The original walruses consisted of three parts, all made of terra-cotta: a head and two tusks held in place by steel rods inserted into a bonding compound. Rumor two: An earthquake in 1949 rattled the heads so vigorously that tusks fell out. The reality: No walruses lost any teeth after the quake, but all of the tusks were replaced in 1982. Unfortunately, the grout used by the installers to hold the newly molded urethane tusks in place expanded when wet, which eventually cracked the heads. In 1997, 13 of the original 27 heads had to be replaced. All of the 1982 tusks remained.

The building's color scheme derives from polychrome terra-cotta, which involves firing color directly into the clay and not painting it on. And, at one time, a terra-cotta polar bear stood at the building's entrance though it disappeared under mysterious circumstances.

Continue west on Cherry Street to 2nd Avenue, and cross to the northwest corner. Across the street to the south is the Broderick Building (615 2nd Avenue).

❾ In 1890, William Bailey, a native of Harrisburg, Pennsylvania, hired the architectural firm of Charles Willard Saunders and Edwin Walker Houghton to design one of the few all-sandstone commercial buildings in the city. The gray stone comes from the Tenino quarries 10 miles south of Olympia. Variously known as the Broderick Building, Bailey Building, and Harrisburg Block, the six-story structure was described as a "symphony in stone" when completed in 1892.

Broderick Building

WALK 5

OPTIONAL SIDE TRIP: MORE FACES IN STONE

From the intersection of Cherry and 2nd Avenue, walk two blocks south on 2nd to Yesler Way. Cross Yesler, turn right, and walk half a block to the red sandstone and brick Interurban Building (157 Yesler Way at Occidental Avenue S).

Originally known as the Seattle National Bank (1 on map), the building earned the name Interurban sometime after 1902, when the Tacoma Interurban (an electric railway that ran from Tacoma through the Green River valley to Seattle) terminated on this block. The train stopped running in 1928, but the name persisted. The building's architect, John Parkinson, designed many schools in Seattle though he would achieve more fame in Los Angeles for buildings such as City Hall and Union Station. This Romanesque-style structure is unusual in Seattle for its use of the red Lyons Sandstone from Manitou Springs, Colorado.

The building has two entrances. To access the bank, customers originally entered at the corner of Yesler and Occidental Avenue S, where a massive lion's head formed the keystone of the arch. It is unclear whether the toothy beast was supposed to intimidate or inspire you. Those who walked in the main entry on Yesler had an equally memorable encounter—grotesques, or faces, carved into the capitals on either side of the doors. Curiously, another face looms out from a sandstone medallion, about 20 feet up on the south edge of the Occidental side of the building. (I have not found any information about why the faces were carved or whether they were based on anyone in particular.)

If you want to see one more human face, and one that may be noticed even less often, walk three blocks south to S Jackson Street, turn right, and continue almost to 1st Avenue and a flight of stairs. Above the subterranean doorway (2 on map), sculptor John H. Geise chiseled a head into the sandstone. Geise lived in the basement apartment in the late 1960s.

Walk north on 1st Avenue to Cherry Street. Turn right, or east, to return to the northwest corner of 2nd and Cherry.

Others have called it imposing and architecturally advanced, but what most fail to note are the 78 grotesques covering the horizontal moldings on the third and fourth floors. To see them best, you will need binoculars. About 5 inches tall, the carvings include dragons, Vikings, bull- and pig-faced heads, and grimacing, elaborately mustachioed, and astonished faces. John Ruskin in Volume 3 of *Modern Painters* wrote: "A fine grotesque is the expression, in a moment, by a series of symbols thrown together in bold and fearless connection, of truths which it would have taken a long time to express in any verbal way, and of which the connection is left for the beholder to work out for himself...." Unfortunately, no contemporary documentation exists for why such figures adorn an office building in downtown Seattle.

Walk north one block on 2nd to Columbia Street, cross to the north side, turn right, and walk one half block up. Across the street is 215 Columbia.

⑩ One of Seattle's stranger structures, the former Seattle Chamber of Commerce Building (1924) is modeled after twelfth-century churches in the Piedmont/Lombardy region of Italy. The multihued cast concrete is supposed to be reminiscent of medieval cut stone. (Cast stone was made to look like real stone and generally incorporated cement, sand, and gravel.) Architect Harlan Thomas, who had lived and traveled throughout Europe, brought his innovative, eclectic style to other buildings in Seattle, including the Sorrento Hotel and the Corner Market Building at Pike Place Market.

However, neither of those buildings incorporate the unusual elements of the Chamber Building. To the left of the front door is a panel depicting Native Americans, each minimally clad and performing "primitive" skills. Opposite is a panel in which a modern man demonstrates his own skills and fashion sense. Also note the small faces peering out of the unusually fluted columns and the winged lions flanking the archway. But to see the most fanciful array of creatures, look up to the frieze. The urban bestiary includes locals such as a duck, pelicans, mountain lions, bears, whales, and an eagle, as well as hippocamps (horses with fish tails) and gazelles.

As you may have noticed, most of these carvings and terra-cotta images are on Seattle's older buildings. Several factors account for this. In particular, ornamentation and its allusions to Classical architecture helped provide an air of gravitas to a young city seeking to make a mark. In addition, Beaux Arts and Art Deco architecture, with their focus on elaborate details, were the popular style during the first half of the 1900s when many of these buildings were constructed.

Seattle also benefited from what we might now call a "local building" movement. The region's abundant, glacially derived clay enabled local firms to develop factories that produced terra-cotta. The factories in turn worked with local artisans to craft the elaborate designs. The same idea applied

The Seaboard Building, 4th Avenue and Pike Street

with the local sandstone, which was most likely carved by people who lived in the region. This stands in contrast to much of the later architecture in downtown buildings, which relied on imported, typically unornamented stone. As happens so often as cities grow, the bigger Seattle became, the more it turned away from its local connections. The abundant carvings and terra cotta forms on Seattle buildings are beautiful reminders of the city's historic relationship to its surroundings.

6

Regrades and the International District

SHAPING A LANDSCAPE OF DIVERSITY

Explore radical changes to the city's topography in a richly diverse neighborhood.

DISTANCE	1.8 miles
START/END	North side of King Street Station, on S Jackson Street between 2nd Avenue S Extension and 3rd Avenue S
NOTES	This walk passes twice under Interstate 5, which can be noisy. There is one relatively steep up and down and a gentle climb from 7th Avenue to 12th Avenue.

Prior to World War II, what we now call the International District (ID) was known as Chinatown and Japantown, or Nihonmachi. Chinatown centered on S King Street from 5th Avenue up to 8th Avenue with the core of Japantown between 5th and 7th Avenues and S Jackson and S Washington Streets. Jackson was the unofficial dividing line. Within this area, a Filipino community also developed around Maynard Avenue and

Chinatown Gate, dedicated February 9, 2008

75

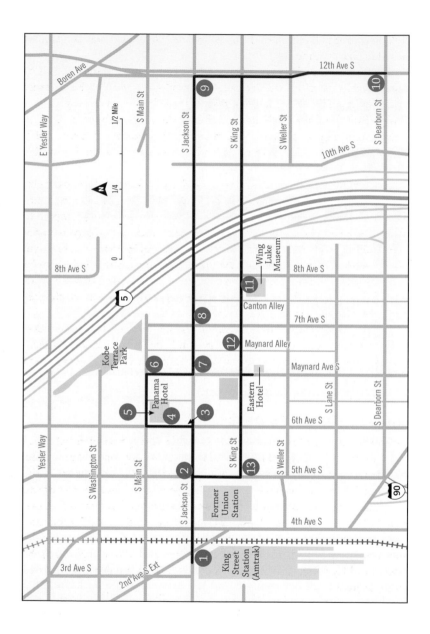

12th Ave S

S Jackson St

S King St

S Weller St

10th Ave S

S Dearborn St

Boren Ave

S Main St

1/2 Mile

E Yesler Way

1/4

8th Ave S

0

5

8th Ave S

Wing Luke Museum

11

Canton Alley

7th Ave S

8

Kobe Terrace Park

12

Maynard Alley

6

7

Maynard Ave S

Panama Hotel

Eastern Hotel

S Lane St

S Dearborn St

5

4

3

6th Ave S

Yesler Way

S Washington St

S Main St

S King St

S Jackson St

2

13

S Weller St

5th Ave S

90

Former Union Station

4th Ave S

3rd Ave S

1

King Street Station (Amtrak)

2nd Ave S Ext

9

10

S Weller Street. And finally, Jackson and 12th Avenue S was the soul of Seattle's jazz community.

The ID was also where two of Seattle's most significant landscape altering projects took place: the Jackson Street (1907–9) and Dearborn Street (1909–12) regrades. Although not nearly as well known as the regrades of Denny Hill, the projects completely altered the neighborhood by cutting down a high ridge and moving four million cubic yards of sediment, which was used to create 85 acres of made land in the tideflats of the Duwamish River.

The driving force behind the two regrades was Seattle's legendary city engineer R. H. Thomson, who wanted to establish less challenging east–west access from the waterfront to Rainier Valley. He had been prompted to start the regrades because of growth in the valley, which had become more populated as people moved there for agriculture and industry and to live in Columbia City. When residents asked the city to bypass the high ridge by excavating two tunnels under Jackson, Thomson countered that eliminating the topographic obstruction via regrading would create a much cheaper and more efficient means to open up Rainier Valley.

Despite the physical and demographic changes in the International District, many linkages to its early history still exist. These include old businesses, a pre-regrade building or two, and arguably the clearest expression of Seattle's propensity to alter the landscape.

Start in the plaza on the north side of King Street Station. Look over the low wall on the east side of the plaza to the train tracks below.

❶ Imagine this location in the 1880s. Instead of being on pavement above the train tracks, you would have stood in a protean landscape. At low tide, you would have been 30 feet below your present location on the mud of the Duwamish River tideflats, and at high tide, you would have been under 10 to 15 feet of water. Above you would have been a wooden trestle that carried Jackson Street across the northern edge of the tideflats. To the east, Jackson would have ascended nearly 200 feet in a half mile to a north–south trending ridge that connected to Beacon Hill. (For comparison, the tower of today's train station is 247 feet high.) This was the ridge removed by the regrades.

Walk east on S Jackson Street to 5th Avenue S. Cross to the northeast corner.

HOW TO RAISE A BUILDING

Workers would have raised the Buty Building with jackscrews (like a modern car jack) and cribs, or wood pallets. They would have begun by first inserting iron beams under the building and then placing the jackscrews under the beams. Listening to signal whistles, each worker would have turned the screws to lift the building, placed support cribbing, and repeated until the building reached its new elevation. No records exist for the Buty, but when workers raised the Eagles Hall (7th Avenue and Pine Street) 14 feet in 1908, they needed 50 hours and 24 minutes; it occurred so smoothly that people in the building continued to play pool and billiards during the process.

❷ You just passed by the former Union Station, which served the Union Pacific Railroad and the Chicago, Milwaukee, St. Paul, and Pacific Railroad. Confusingly, King Street Station was originally called Union Depot because it served both the Great Northern and Northern Pacific Railroads.

Across Jackson from where you stand is an unusual structure. In 1901 Frank Buty built his eponymous three-story brick building (his name is above the arched entryway). Six years later he had to lift the building during the regrade because Thomson wanted Jackson Street to have a consistent, relatively gentle grade, which required dirt from higher spots on Jackson to be moved to lower spots to raise the land up to a new level. For example, enough fill was added at 5th Avenue that Buty's building would have been left 18 feet below grade. To the south and east, King and Weller Streets required even more fill, with about 30 feet added along 6th Avenue. After raising his original structure to the new street level, Buty added an addition to the east, which accounts for the strange bi-level roof.

One additional note as you walk up Jackson. Look at the street signs installed by the city in 2013. On the north side of the street they are written in Japanese, using katakana characters (used primarily for transcription of foreign language words into Japanese) for the street name and kanji (Chinese characters used for Japanese writing) for the word *street*. Because Jackson was the original dividing line between Chinatown and Japantown, the south-side signs are in Chinese.

Walk east and cross to the east side of 6th Avenue S. Continue east a short way to the storefront of the Kobo at Higo Gallery.

❸ This two-story brick building is a direct link to Seattle's former thriving Nihonmachi. In 1909 Japanese immigrants Sanzo and Matsuyo Murakami opened the Higo 10 Cent Store (named for Sanzo's birthplace) on S Weller Street. The business prospered selling Japanese and American products, and in 1932 the Murakamis moved to a new building constructed to their specifications at Jackson and 6th.

The Murakamis had arrived in Seattle as part of a wave of Japanese immigration that began after the 1882 Chinese Exclusion Act prohibited Chinese from entering the country. By 1890, 300 or so Japanese lived in Seattle, where they worked primarily as manual laborers on railroads and in logging camps and canneries. The population reached 4,000 in 1900 and nearly 8,000 in 1920. Because of discrimination and racism (Washington State's Alien Land Act of 1921 prevented Japanese from owning or renting land), most Japanese lived in and around Japantown, which centered on 6th Avenue S and S Main Street. As David Takami wrote in *Divided Destiny: A History of Japanese Americans in Seattle*, "Growing up in Nihonmachi in the 1920s provided a wonderful blend of Japan and America." One could play baseball, bathe at one of several Japanese bathhouses, walk the streets hearing only Japanese spoken, or eat hotdogs, baloney sandwiches, and *kintoki* (shaved ice with beans and syrup).

This changed abruptly on February 19, 1942, when President Franklin Roosevelt signed Executive Order 9066, the law that incarcerated 120,000 Japanese Americans in internment camps throughout the western United States. In April they were forced to leave behind their homes, businesses, and livelihoods. They were taken first to "Camp Harmony" in Puyallup, and then to the camps in California and Idaho.

The Higo 10 Cent continued to be an essential part of Japantown until World War II. Before leaving the city, the Murakamis, like many others in Japantown, boarded up their store. Fortunately for the Murakamis, two tenants in their building, Julius Blumenthal and his half brother, Maurice Zimmer, watched over the building throughout the war. The Murakamis returned on January 22, 1945, and reopened the store, which became a center for returning Japanese. Higo Variety Store, as the children renamed it in 1957, stayed in business until 2003. A year later, John Bisbee and Binko

Chiong-Bisbee opened their Kobo at Higo Gallery. Within the gallery, they sell art supplies and artwork and have built a space dedicated to the story of the Murakamis and their store. It is well worth going inside and seeing the historic cabinets, display cases, and artifacts.

Walk back to 6th, turn right, and walk north about halfway up the block.

❹ Built in 1914, the Northern Pacific (or NP) Hotel, was one of more than 125 Japanese-managed hotels in Seattle in the 1920s. Built for working-men, these hotels offered rooms for single men and shared bathrooms. The rooms might have a hotplate, but most residents ate in one of the many restaurants in Nihonmachi and Chinatown. In 1994, the hotel was restored and adapted for low-income housing. The small wooden building across the street was the annex of the former Main Street School, which served many of Seattle's first-generation Japanese and Chinese children.

Continue up 6th to S Main Street, turn right, and walk east to the entrance to the Panama Hotel.

❺ Few establishments were more important to the pre–World War II Japanese community than the Panama Hotel, which opened in 1910 and still operates as a hotel and cafe. Designed by one of the first Japanese architects in the country, Sabro Ozasa, the hotel had 94 single-occupancy rooms, a bookstore, dentist, and sushi shop, as well as a Japanese-style public bathhouse, or *sento,* named Hashidate-Yu. Though not open for business, it is one of two surviving sentos in the United States.

During their incarceration, many local Japanese families stored their belongings in the hotel's basement. After the war, owner Takashi Hori came back to reopen his hotel. He attempted to return trunks and suitcases to their owners, but many former residents did not return to Seattle or did not want their old belongings. The abandoned goods remained in the basement until 1985 when the Hori family sold the hotel to Jan Johnson, who created a small museum that features the items accompanied by historic photographs. The hotel's cafe provides access to the museum. The Panama Hotel was placed on the National Register of Historic Places in 2006 and named a "National Treasure" in 2015 by the National Trust for Historic Preservation.

Continue east on S Main to Maynard Avenue S, and cross to the east side of the street.

❻ To the north is Danny Woo Community Garden and the Kobe Terrace Park. Originally created by the construction of Interstate 5, the small park was named in 1974 to honor Seattle's Sister City in Japan. If you wander up through the community gardens, you can find a diverse collection of plants, uninterrupted views south to Mount Rainier, and a 200-year-old Yukimi-doro stone lantern.

To the south is the Maynard Green Street, built in 2010 as part of Seattle's Green Street program, which was established to enhance open space and pedestrian circulation. Combining public art with a water filtration system, the Maynard project incorporates rooftop runoff that enters a cistern before flowing down Maynard into planters. The planters also function as benches to aid walkers ascending and descending the steep street.

Imagine this location before the regrade. It would have looked somewhat similar to what you see now with a steep hill to the north and a steep drop off to the south. The main difference is that the regrade lowered each of the nearby streets (Main, Maynard, and Jackson) by about 25 feet. It may seem odd that the regrade left behind steep streets; the goal was not to improve north–south travel but to make it easier to travel east–west.

Walk down (south) along the Maynard Green to S Jackson Street (grade of 15 percent). Cross over to the south side of the street. Turn around to look back at the buildings on the north side of Jackson.

❼ On the northwest corner is another unusual building, or buildings. The bottom brick structure with several storefronts was built in 1910. Atop it are a twin-gabled structure, which was originally the Japanese Baptist Church built circa 1893, and a flat-roofed building, the former Jackson Hotel. During the regrade, this corner was excavated to a lower elevation. To protect the church during the work, house mover Lemuel Gullett placed the building on a 30-foot-high stack of pallets, or cribbing. After the brick building was finished, Gullet lowered the church onto its new foundation. It later became the Havana Hotel. In other words, the former gabled church is about 10 feet lower than its elevation before the regrade when it was at the original ground level. At the same time, the Jackson Hotel was also moved from its former location, one block west at 6th and Jackson and set atop the brick substructure. A 1984 restoration of the entire building complex converted it to low-income housing and retail.

HOUSE MOVERS' DEPARTMENT

SEATTLE CITY DIRECTORY (1911)   1685

L. B. GULLETT
EXPERIENCED

HOUSE MOVER

House Moving, Raising, Lowering
and Wrecking

HEAVY SHORING FOR STORE FRONTS

Brick or Concrete Foundations, Retaining Walls, Sidewalks, Etc.
HOUSES BOUGHT AND SOLD

2041 Westlake Ave., Seattle, Wash.

Telephone: Sunset, Main 2711

Advertisement in Seattle City Directory
featuring Japanese Baptist Church, 1911

Continue east up Jackson Street to 7th Avenue S.

❽ Imagine standing in 1905 where Interstate 5 now runs. You would be 60 feet higher than the level of the modern highway atop a one-block-wide ridge that sloped gently up to the north. On the somewhat steep west side were homes and rows of apartments, which continued over the hill. Crossing east over the ridge, Jackson dropped down a less steep slope that leveled off at 12th Avenue before crossing a small creek at 14th. And going up Jackson Street was the Jackson Street trolley, which ran every 10 minutes.

Between 1908 and 1910, workers washed away the ridge and lowered Jackson by 85 feet at 9th down to the present level of Jackson. (For more information, see Walk 2.) Today Interstate 5 is about 30 feet above Jackson, which rises at a steady 5.1 percent between 4th and 12th. Pre-regrade Jackson had slopes as steep as 18 percent. If you look north up 7th from Jackson to Main, you are seeing an 11 percent grade. With a slope in places of 19.5 percent, nearby King Street was so steep there wasn't even a road, just a dirt path up the ridge.

After passing under the freeway, you enter Little Saigon, long the center of Seattle's Vietnamese community. Refugees began to arrive in the city following the fall of Saigon in 1975 and soon developed a thriving neighborhood that expanded east out of Chinatown. More recently, Cambodian and Laotian communities have also made the area their home.

The next part of this walk takes you through a section of the International District that has suffered from the construction of Interstate 5. There have been attempts to make it more hospitable, such as the bold yellow and red columns under the freeway, but it still retains a gritty feel. The main

Jackson Street Regrade, 1908, 11th Avenue S and S King Street

reason is to head up Jackson to the Dr. Jose Rizal Bridge to experience one of the most dramatic examples of how regrades changed Seattle's topography.

Walk east on S Jackson Street to 12th Avenue S.

❾ You have reached the edge of the regrade and are now at a modern elevation equal to its historic elevation. This intersection was "where Seattle jazz was born and where it flowered, from the late teens until the 1960s," wrote Paul de Barros in *Jackson Street after Hours: The Roots of Jazz in Seattle.* Two of the best known clubs were the Alhambra, also known as the Black and Tan because it admitted blacks and whites, and the Entertainers Club. Both were on the southeast corner in the building that still stands. By the late 1940s, more than 30 nightclubs were on Jackson. The scene not only attracted nationally known performers such as Jelly Roll Morton, Oscar Holden, Duke Ellington, Charlie Parker, and Count Basie, but it also fostered Quincy Jones, Ernestine Anderson, and Ray Charles.

Turn right, and walk south on the west side of 12th Avenue S and out to the middle of the Dr. Jose Rizal Bridge.

⑩ If you had walked south on 12th Avenue in 1908 before the regrade, you would have been at about the same elevation as the bridge but on a road that crossed the ridge that connected to Beacon Hill. Facing Elliott Bay from this point, you would have looked abruptly down into a small valley. On the other side of the valley, the Dearborn slope continued steeply toward the bay, losing about 100 feet in two blocks. To the east, the ridge dropped precipitously before leveling off at Rainier Avenue.

This obstruction troubled the good citizens of Rainier Valley, who felt that Dearborn Street's 15 to 18 percent grades up and over the frustrating topography made it difficult to travel to and from downtown Seattle. Not only was the ridge hard for residents to traverse, but it thwarted the valley's logging and manufacturing industries, which needed easy access to railroads or at least easy means of transporting goods to rail.

To solve this transportation problem and to improve access to Rainier Valley, city engineer R. H. Thomson proposed to regrade Dearborn from 6th Avenue S to Rainier Avenue. Dearborn would be widened from 66 to 90 feet with the deepest cut of 108 feet at Dearborn and 12th. The result was the completely artificial valley below you.

Return north on 12th to S King Street. Turn left, or west, and walk down the south side of King under I-5 toward Chinatown. One half block past 8th Avenue S, at 719 S King, is the Wing Luke Museum. It is well worth a visit, even if you have been there previously.

⑪ You have now entered what is arguably Seattle's third Chinatown. Chun Ching Hock was Seattle's first Chinese immigrant in 1860. By 1876, about 300 Chinese lived in town, mostly around what is now Occidental Park. Many started out working in restaurants, laundries, and hotels, but hard manual labor soon became their primary occupations, with Chun Ching Hock acting as their labor contractor.

As with the Japanese, the Chinese experienced extreme racism, which culminated in one of the more reprehensible events in Seattle history. In November 1885, labor and civic leaders pressured the city's Chinese to get out of town by telling them that if they didn't leave potentially uncontrollable violence would ensue. One hundred and fifty fled by boat and train. Three months later, citizen mobs invaded the Chinese section of town and violently forced everyone to the waterfront, where 200 of Seattle's 350 remaining Chinese were put on a boat and expelled from town.

WING LUKE MUSEUM OF THE ASIAN
PACIFIC AMERICAN EXPERIENCE

Originally opened in a small storefront on 8th Avenue, the Wing Luke Museum
honors Seattle's first person of color on the Seattle City Council and the first
Asian American elected to public office in the Pacific Northwest. Wing Luke was
born in China in 1925, and arrived in Seattle with his parents when he was six. He
was student body president at Roosevelt High School, received a law degree from
the University of Washington, and won his election in 1962. Unfortunately, he died
three years later in a plane crash at the age of 40.

The museum moved to its present facility in 2008 with a renewed focus on telling the story of Asian Pacific Americans through exhibits and community outreach.
It is the only museum in the United States devoted to the Pan-Asian experience.

By 1890, however, enough Chinese had returned to Seattle to form a
new community, centered on S Washington Street between 2nd and 4th
Avenues S. Oriented around the *tong*, or family association, the new
Chinatown provided most of the services anyone would need from lodging to banking to restaurants to mail service. Only one building remains
from this Chinatown, the Chin Gee Hee Building (built in 1890) at 200 2nd
Avenue S Extension, which housed Chin Gee Hee's labor contracting and
import/export businesses. (To see the building, walk north on 2nd Avenue
S Extension from the walk's starting point.)

Chinatown moved again following the Jackson Street regrade, when the
Kong Yick Investment Company, organized by entrepreneur and commu-
nity leader Goon Dip, built several brick buildings on S King Street between
8th Avenue S and Maynard Avenue S. This area soon became the center of
Seattle's third Chinatown. The Wing Luke Museum is in one of the Kong
Yick buildings.

Near to the Wing Luke are two unusual features of Chinatown. Canton
Alley, directly west of the museum, is one of a handful of named alleys in
the city. Like the nearby Maynard Alley, Canton developed in part because
of overcrowding. As more and more people moved into the neighborhood,
builders exploited every possible space, and alleys that weren't being used
provided a good place for people to live or open shops.

To see the second feature, look up at the building across the street from the Wing Luke. The recessed balcony indicates a tong, which often maintained elaborate buildings with lodging, commercial activities, and social venues. Balconies such as these originated in south China, the home of many of Seattle's Chinese immigrants. (For a regrade perspective, compare the intersection of 7th and King, which was lowered about 45 feet, roughly equal to the height of the building with the balcony.)

Continue west on S King Street toward 6th Avenue S. Several stops that you'll pass by on the walk to 6th are described here, but only the first stop is numbered.

⓬ Taking up half of the north side of King past 7th is the Goon Dip Building, or Milwaukee Hotel (whose name may allude to the Chicago, Milwaukee, St. Paul, and Pacific Railroad, also known as the Milwaukee Road). The hotel opened in 1911 as one of the first and among the most prominent buildings in the new Chinatown. Rooms cost $3.00 per week and included hot and cold running water and access to long-distance telephones.

At the next intersection, turn left and walk one half block south on Maynard Avenue S to the Eastern Hotel. Completed in 1911, it became a center for the Filipino community that developed around the hotel. About 1,600 Filipinos lived in Seattle by 1930. As with other Asian immigrants, they faced discrimination from white residents and the government. One of the hotel's most famous short-term residents was the great Filipino writer and poet Carlos Bulosan, whose book *America Is in the Heart* tells of the Filipino experience in the United States. The building displays some of the most lovely brickwork in the area. Return to King and continue west on it.

Just past Maynard Avenue S on the north side of the street is Hing Hay Park, which the city bought in 1972 and opened to the public in 1974. A year later, the pagoda, a gift from the City Council of Taipei, Taiwan, arrived in 57 cartons. It was assembled on site.

On the southwest corner of 6th Avenue S is a kiosk that focuses on Filipinos in Seattle, and on King is an elaborate gate completed in 2008.

Continue west on King one block to 5th Avenue S.

⓭ On the southeast corner of 5th and King is the Publix Building, which was built in 1927–28 and remodeled in 2015–16. What is not visible are the building's two levels of basement, a main basement with an 18-foot ceiling and under that a sub-basement that bottoms out at about the level of the tracks of the light-rail station across the street. In addition, a delivery window opens into the sub-basement, an indication that ground level used to be more than 20 feet under the modern street level.

The subterranean delivery window alludes to the beginning of the walk and the tideflats, the historic boundary of which extended east to what is now 5th Avenue. The modern train and light-rail tracks enter their stations below the grade of the nearby streets because they run at the level of trestles that originally brought trains across the tideflats into the city. An early pre-regrade era of tideflat filling initially put the tracks on solid ground, followed by the Dearborn and Jackson regrades, which raised up the streets around the tracks.

That the Chinese and Japanese and Filipinos settled in this neighborhood is not surprising. Marginalized people were often relegated to land perceived to be inferior, whether it was the tideflats of the Duwamish River, beaches along bluffs, or the regrade districts. They moved to these landscapes not necessarily because they wanted to but because they were the only places available to them or affordable. However, as these communities grew and became established, they have contributed to making Seattle a more robust city that has benefited in innumerable cultural and economic ways from its diverse populations.

Turn right, or north, on 6th, walk one block to S Jackson Street, and turn left to return to the starting point.

THEATRE.   4. CENTRAL SCHOOL MADISON ST. No 200.

Madison Street

ELLIOTT BAY TO LAKE WASHINGTON

Walk a roller coaster of hills following the only street
that connects Seattle's two largest bodies of water.

DISTANCE	3.7 miles, one way
STARTING POINT	Alaskan Way and Madison Street
ENDING POINT	Madison Street at Lake Washington
NOTES	Metro Bus route 11 goes directly from the ending point to within a few blocks of the starting point. This is the most hilly walk in the book with more than 1,000 feet of elevation change, including a steady rise of more than 300 feet in the first mile. You could do this walk in reverse, but doing so is less interesting because I include less information about the Lake Washington end of the walk.

No other street in Seattle can match Madison Street's claim to fame. It is
the only street that runs continuously from Elliott Bay to Lake Washington. Madison was also one of the first named streets in Seattle. On May
23, 1853, Arthur Denny platted a section of the "Town of Seattle," naming
Madison for the fourth president and Marion (and James Street) for his
brother, James Marion Denny.

    Long before Madison Street officially ran from bay to lake, John J. McGilvra bought 323 acres on the shore of Lake Washington for $1.25/acre in 1864.

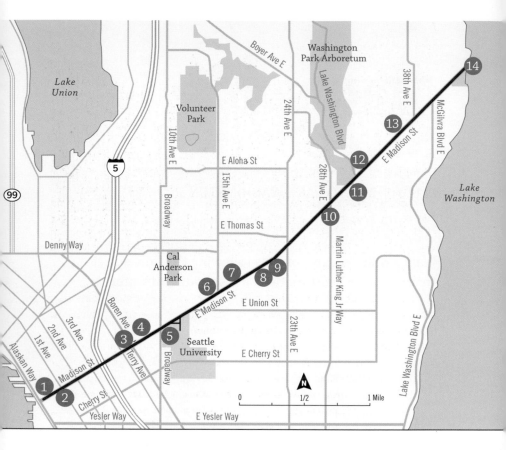

Just south of modern Madison Park, he built a house, named Laurel Shade, and became Seattle's original long-distance commuter when he hired a Native crew to cut a 3.5-mile path from downtown to his property. Total cost of this path was $1,500 in gold coin. We don't know how long Seattle's first commute took, but journalist Thomas Prosch described the route in 1871 as "almost as crooked as the letter S, and up and down, rough, and little more than a trail in width." He added that east of 6th Avenue, dense timber replaced houses. To ease his commute and to promote the real estate he hoped to sell, McGilvra later established the Madison Street Cable Railway, which in 1890 began to carry passengers from Elliott Bay to the lake.

Looking east up Madison Street, 1891

Not only does this walk allow you to trace Seattle's earliest commute, but it also illustrates the city's economic geography. You start downtown in the urban core, proceed up to its first tony housing area, pass through an early African American community, and descend into a shopping enclave before going by one of Seattle's wealthiest neighborhoods and ending at another one.

Madison also provides a visceral way to get a better sense of the ridge and valley system carved during the last ice age. Starting at Elliott Bay, Madison rises up one glacial ridge, descends into the valley at 12th Avenue E, ascends to Second, or Renton, Hill (at 17th Avenue), drops nearly 300 feet into Madison Valley, and rises once more before a last descent to freshwater.

Start on the waterfront at Alaskan Way and Madison Street.

❶ Madison Street was the north–south dividing line between the city's two historic seawalls. The first—from S Washington Street to Madison— was completed in 1916 and consisted of an unreinforced concrete wall supported by wood pilings. North of Madison, the wall was made of pre-cast concrete panels, steel-sheet pilings, a horizontal wooden platform, and wooden pilings. Workers filled in the area behind the seawall with sediment from the Cedar River. Due to a lack of funding, the construction of the northern section was not started until 1934. It was completed two years later.

Construction of the modern seawall began in 2013. Unlike its predecessors, the new design takes into account seismic concerns, climate change–induced sea level rise, and habitat for native plants and animals. It also avoids the use of wood, which suffers from infestations of inveterate invertebrates.

Thanks to the old seawall, you are walking across made land, or land created with fill material, for the first 700 feet of this route. Sediment from the Cedar River was transported by barge and dumped behind the seawall in 1936, adding to a more heterogeneous mix of rubber, glass, wood chips, concrete, slag, and bricks deposited by private citizens. Ground core samples around Madison Street also reveal debris from Seattle's Great Fire of 1889, including the remnants of a bottle of Lydia E. Pinkham's Vegetable Compound, a remedy for "female complaints" that contained about 20 percent alcohol.

The first place you reach natural land is 1st Avenue, originally known as Front Street for its location on the waterfront. In 1878, the street was the site of Seattle's first official regrade when contractor Frank Edwards smoothed out the undulating roadway. He also made a clear separation between land and water by building a sort of seawall. Up to 27 feet high, it consisted of horizontal logs anchored to logs driven perpendicularly into the embankment.

Walk east on the south side of Madison to 1st Avenue.

❷ On both sides of 1st Avenue are Seattle's two federal buildings. The classic Art Deco structure, called the Old Federal Building, was designed in 1931 and completed in 1933. Across the street, the Henry M. Jackson Federal Building was built between 1971 and 1974. On its east side, on 2nd Avenue, is a sandstone arch from the site's original structure, the Burke Building, along with red terra-cotta elements from the earlier building.

Seattle's Great Fire of 1889 started on the southwest corner of 1st. (For more information, see Walk 3.) At the time, Front Street was still on the shoreline though two sets of train tracks ran on trestles that rose out of the water west of Front. The Columbia and Puget Sound Railroad curved inland from Yesler to almost Front, and the Seattle Lake Shore and Eastern Railway was slightly west of what is now Western Avenue.

Seattle Public Library, Central Branch, 1916

Begin the climb of Madison Street, pausing at 2nd Avenue to see the arch and terra-cotta. Cross Interstate 5 and continue to Terry Avenue. The following section includes descriptions of short stops along the way to Terry, where there is a longer stop. (Only the last of these stops is numbered on the map.)

❸ From 3rd to 4th Avenues is the steepest downtown block at 19 percent grade. The tall glass-clad building on 4th was Seattle's tallest building from 1969 to 1985. Originally known as the Seattle First National Bank, or Seafirst Building, the uniformly black skyscraper has long unofficially been called "the box the Space Needle came in."

On the northeast corner of 4th is at least the sixth building to house the downtown Seattle Public Library. In 1891, the first official library's first home was in the Occidental Building in Pioneer Square, but the library did not remain there long—it bounced around to a variety of buildings, including Henry Yesler's mansion, until it found a permanent location on this corner in 1906 in an Andrew Carnegie–funded building. Five decades later that classic structure succumbed to the wrecking ball. Its replacement was open from 1960 to 2001. On May 23, 2004, the new library designed by Dutch architect Rem Koolhaas opened to the public. You either love it or hate it.

Across 5th is the William Kenzo Nakamura United States Courthouse. Built in 1940, it was the first sole purpose courthouse in the western United States. It was renamed in 2001 after Private First Class Nakamura, a Seattle native whose family was sent to an internment camp. Nakamura later joined the Army and died in Italy in 1944 while protecting his platoon. He was awarded the Congressional Medal of Honor in 2000.

The Sorrento Hotel (stop 3 on the map) at Terry Avenue opened in 1909 as one of the first luxury residential hotels in the city. Designed by Harlan Thomas, a well-regarded but somewhat eclectic architect, the hotel offered great views by putting tearooms and the main dining room on the top floor. Over the decades it has been renovated and updated to retain the grand style it had when it first opened though it is no longer a long-term residential hotel.

Continue up Madison to Minor Avenue.

❹ By 1876, about 70 people lived on First Hill, which is defined in *Tradition and Change on Seattle's First Hill* as the area north of Yesler Way, east of 6th Avenue (now I-5), west of Broadway and Boren Avenues, and south of E Pike Street. Early residents worked in the trades, but the hill soon became the domain of Seattle's most august citizens, who would hold "at home" days on Wednesday, "when dainty tables were spread and tea and gossip served," wrote Sophie Frye Bass, one of Arthur Denny's granddaughters. First Hill also became the home of wealthy residents' social clubs, such as the University Men's Club, the Sunset Club, and the Seattle Tennis Club. The northwest corner of this intersection is the approximate location of the tennis club's first tournament site.

A more modern name for First is Pill Hill in reference to its many hospitals. The Sisters of Charity of Providence opened Seattle's first hospital in 1878 at 5th Avenue and Madison. Seven years later Trinity Parish Church established Grace Hospital at Summit Avenue and Union Street.

SEATTLE'S SEVEN HILLS

The idea that Seattle was built on seven hills like ancient Rome has been part of city lore since the early 1900s. These seven hills were Beacon, Capitol, Denny, First, Profanity, Queen Anne, and Renton (aka Second). Some people consider Profanity, or Yesler, where Harborview Hospital stands, to be a shoulder of First Hill and not worthy of hill status, but they are spoilsports. As the city has spread, it has gained more hills, and Magnolia and West Seattle have replaced Renton and Profanity in Seattle's pantheon.

Other small private hospitals opened nearby. Then in 1910 Swedish Hospital began its long-term residence on the hill. Columbus, or Cabrini, Hospital opened in 1916, followed by Virginia Mason in 1920 and Harborview in 1931.

By the early 1900s, First Hill had lost its cachet of exclusiveness as apartment builders known derisively as "dollar doublers" began to move in. Their buildings provided housing for individuals and families. Most buildings were relatively small though the Perry Hotel (now demolished) at Boren Avenue and Madison was eight stories tall with 83 units. By 1915, the golden age of grand homes on First Hill was over. According to historian Paul Dorpat, there were more than 800 residential homes on the hill in 1912 but only 60 by 2013. Four of the elegant great houses remain: Stimson-Green Mansion (1204 Minor Avenue); Dearborn House (1117 Minor Avenue, now the offices of Historic Seattle); Connolly House (1104 Spring Street, now the residence of the archbishop of Seattle); and Stacy House (1004 Boren Avenue, which now houses the University Club).

Continue along Madison to Broadway.

❺ What is now Seattle University began in 1891 when Fathers Victor Garrand and Adrian Sweere founded Immaculate Conception as a day school. Seven years later Sweere changed the school's focus to higher education, renaming it Seattle College. The oldest structure is the Garrand Building, which was erected in 1894. It now houses Seattle University's School of Nursing. After struggling with low attendance during World War I, the college bought Adelphia College (home of today's Seattle Preparatory

School) on Interlaken Boulevard. Seattle College stayed on Interlaken for a dozen years before moving back to its original Broadway campus in 1931 and being renamed Seattle University in 1948.

If you want a nice side trip, continue east on Madison on the south side of the street to the first entrance to the Seattle University Campus. Enter the campus, and turn left. Proceed down the walkway to just past Hunthausen Hall, and turn right, or south, to reach the Chapel of St. Ignatius, a fantastic little building designed by Steven Holl, who has written that the building symbolizes "seven bottles of light in a stone box." Return north to Madison.

Continue on Madison to its intersection with E Pike Street.

❻ You are standing between two historic religious institutions. The red brick building with the square tower to the north is First African Methodist Episcopal Church (FAME), the oldest African American church in Washington State. Its first members began meeting in each other's homes in 1886, and four years later bought a lot at what was then Jones Street and Madison. The location was roughly the western edge of one of the largest concentrations of black homeowners in Seattle, which stretched along Madison to about what is now Martin Luther King Jr. Way E. The present FAME building dates from 1912.

East up Pike Street is the concrete Temple De Hirsch Sinai, Seattle's second Jewish congregation. Organized in 1899 and named for Baron Maurice de Hirsch, a German-born English philanthropist, the congregation started its first temple in 1901 at Boylston and Marion Streets. It was never finished. Eight years later the congregation dedicated a new building at 15th Avenue and Union Street, a location designed to attract people from the thriving Jewish neighborhood on Yesler Way between 12th and 20th Avenues, as well as a growing community on Capitol Hill. In 1960, congregants built the present-day sanctuary. The old synagogue, except for the columns, was demolished in 1992.

Because Madison cuts across the normal grid of Seattle streets, it has created many little triangular spaces, some too small to develop beyond odd islands of pavement, others large enough to become blocks, and a few in-between sizes that morphed into green spaces. Such was the fate of the odd, tree-lined triangular space across the street, which was acquired by the city in 1901 and is now known as McGilvra Place Park.

Continue on Madison to 17th Avenue.

❼ Congratulations—you have reached the summit of another of Seattle's original seven hills. Second, or Renton, Hill honors Captain William Renton, a lumber merchant who arrived in Puget Sound in 1852 and for whom the town of Renton is named. He also purchased this hill that bears his name and logged it, which led to "the sickening sight of all logged-off lands—stumps, raw and splintered; saplings, stripped and bent; earth scarred and torn," wrote Sophie Frye Bass.

As you continue east, look on the north side of Madison, just before 19th Avenue, for a mural of cows. It is an homage to the cows painted in various styles (such as a cubist cow and Jackson Pollock cow) on the former Fratelli's Ice Cream plant, which stood on this corner for more than two decades.

Just about where 20th Avenue intersects, look on the sidewalk for the Madison Poetry Project, a poem in stone written by J. T. Stewart. The poem was put in place at the same time as a pedestrian safety project, designed to slow down cars turning from Madison onto E. Olive Street.

Continue on Madison to 22nd Avenue.

❽ When the Madison Street Cable Railway opened, it included a power house at the southwest corner of this intersection, which turned the cables that pulled the cars. Each of the two six-strand cables was about 20,000 feet long. The one that ran from here to the lake traveled at a speedy 12 miles per hour, and the town section moved along at a slower 10 miles per hour. Gripman Oscar DeFreon told a *Seattle Times* reporter, "We made a big pull up the hill from Western Avenue to the power house on one cable. Then we coasted a few feet with the grip released, and joined the second cable to hold us back down the hill to the lake."

The Madison cable line didn't simply carry passengers between home and office; it also benefited landowners such as McGilvra. An article in *The Street Railway Journal* reported that real-estate advertising placards covered nearly every surface of the cars, including windows, commenting that "The practice cannot be said to add to the beauty of the cars."

Continue one block east to 23rd Avenue.

❾ The city's second African American resident, William Grose, arrived in Seattle in 1860 (its first, Manuel Lopes, had moved there in 1852). After working as a cook, Grose opened a successful restaurant and hotel on the waterfront called Our House. In 1882, he purchased 12 acres near this intersection from Henry Yesler for $1,000 in gold. He initially farmed the land, but when the Great Seattle Fire burned Our House to the ground, Grose moved to his property and built a home, where he lived until his death in 1898. Grose also sold his land to other black families, which helped lead to the development of a large African American community along and south of Madison and down into Madison Valley. His original family home still stands on 24th Avenue.

As you walk down Madison, look for blue-and-white tile street names embedded in the sidewalk. There is one on the south side at E Thomas Street. They are found along Madison, including one with odd lettering at 32nd Avenue E. Marking streets in this manner was popular in the early 20th century, though Seattle's tiles are unusual. Other cities used what are known as encaustic tiles, with each letter pressed and fired into a single tile, but Seattle favored numerous tiny tiles.

Continue down Madison to where Martin Luther King Jr. Way E and 28th Avenue E intersect.

⑩ 28th has been known by various names in its long history. Its original name, Buckius Street, was changed to 28th in 1895 during a widespread renaming of city streets. Later it was renamed Empire Way in honor of railroad magnate James J. Hill, the "empire builder." Empire Way originally ran only in south Seattle and was developed in 1912 to provide better access through Rainier Valley. The name change to Empire occurred in 1958, around the time that the city began to make plans for an Empire Expressway (later known as the R. H. Thomson Expressway), which would have created a four-lane roadway from Rainier Valley to what is now State Route 520. The latest name incarnation was finalized in January 1984, when, after three years of legal battles, Empire Way became Martin Luther King Jr. Way.

Continue on Madison past 29th Avenue, which intersects it from the north, until you reach several handrails.

⑪ A wooden trestle was built in 1890 to carry the Madison Street Cable Railway cars across the valley that is visible on either side of Madison Street. Although the trestle, or bridge, as some called it, carried trolley cars

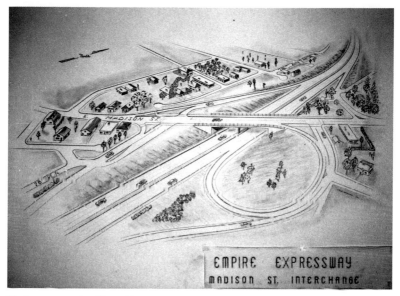

EMPIRE EXPRESSWAY
MADISON ST. INTERCHANGE

Plan for never-completed Empire Expressway, 1960

as often as every two minutes in the summer, newspaper articles describe how it regularly needed repairs. Finally, the city decided in 1924 to fill in the area crossed by the trestle. This did not please the neighbors as the fill consisted of city garbage, but as one health department official told residents, "You are responsible for its [the garbage's] production. You don't want us to dump it at someone else's backdoor, do you?" Apparently they did.

Continue east to Lake Washington Boulevard.

⑫ Although some think that we live in an era that is too bike-centric, consider the early 1900s when there were over 20 bike stores in downtown, one newspaper ran a weekly column devoted to biking news, and approximately one out of every eight Seattleites was a bike rider. For these dedicated riders, the most popular route ran from Lake Union through modern-day Interlaken Park across Madison Street to Madrona Park. When landscape architect John Charles Olmsted arrived in Seattle in 1903, he recognized the future potential of the bike path and incorporated it in his grand plan for interconnected boulevards and parks in Seattle, which ultimately led to the creation of today's modern Lake Washington Boulevard and many of Seattle's parks.

From this point onward, this walk covers less history and is more of a stroll through a beautiful neighborhood. You have now walked 2.7 miles and have another mile to go to reach the lake. This could be a good turn-around point, a place to catch a bus, or a spot to turn north and head through the Washington Park Arboretum. Of course, there is also the temptation of completing a rare geographic feat and going all the way to the lake.

If this temptation wins out, continue up Madison, up the final glacially carved ridge, to the entrance to Broadmoor Golf Club at 36th Avenue E.

⑬ In late 1924, the Puget Mill Company began to run advertisements in the Seattle newspapers about the "only exclusive Golf and Country Club and private residential park" located within a city in the United States. This exclusivity derived in part from covenants that stated that the property could never be used or occupied "by any Hebrew or by any person of the Ethiopian, Malay, or any Asiatic race." Broadmoor was not unique in its blatant discrimination: a University of Washington research project in 2005 and 2006 found 416 deeds and covenants with racial restrictions in Seattle and its suburbs, which forced people of color or a religious minority into specific neighborhoods in the city. Many of these restrictions still appear on covenants though they are no longer used or enforced and are illegal.

A couple of blocks past the Broadmoor's entrance is a large brick house on the north side of Madison. Now the Russian Consulate, it was built in 1910 for liquor entrepreneur Samuel Hyde.

Continue down Madison to Lake Washington.

⑭ You made it! Madison Park opened in 1890 when Judge McGilvra set aside 21 acres for a public playground on the water. It was not a completely benevolent act, as visitors couldn't help but see McGilvra's lots for sale around the park. Just north of the park was the home grounds for Seattle's first professional baseball team—the Seattles—which started playing on May 24, 1890. According to the *Seattle P-I,* baseball "attracts the finest people and is everywhere eminently respectable ... [and] wholly free from the vulgarities which make the race course objectionable." The home team won its first game 11–8.

The lake end of Madison was also important as the departure point for boat travel to the east side. Early boat service was run by private companies; the Curtis family owned the 60-foot *Elfin,* which in 1891 made six round-trips a day between Madison and Kirkland, along with stops at numerous small landings scattered around the lake. One-way fare was a dime. By 1900, public ferry service had begun, but it had to compete with the private runs, which sailed from Madison at least 15 times a day. The building of the floating bridges eliminated the need for boat service and the final ferry run on Lake Washington left Madison Park on August 31, 1950.

Although the elimination of the ferries and the historic trolleys has made Madison less important as a travel corridor in modern Seattle, few streets in Seattle share its unusual mix of history and topography. And no other affords the opportunity to walk from bay to lake.

To return to the beginning of the walk, catch Metro Bus route 11 on the north side of Madison about one-third of a mile west at McGilvra Boulevard E.

Lake Union

CIRCUMNAVIGATING THE CENTER OF THE CITY

Walk a loop around one of the city's
most dynamic landscapes.

DISTANCE	7 miles
START/END	Gas Works Park
NOTES	This is the longest walk in the book. Public restrooms are available at the beginning and in the middle of the walk. If you don't want to complete the circumnavigation, you can catch Metro Bus route 40 along Westlake Avenue N, which takes you across the Fremont Bridge and cuts off about two miles.

Lake Union is a microcosm of the Seattle story. It has seen industries as diverse as steam plants, lumber mills, a gasification plant, and plane building; has served as a dumping ground for everything from ships to dirt from Interstate 5; and has been home to everyone from eccentrics and bohemians to doctors and dot.com executives. And, like many places in Seattle in the past few decades, Lake Union has undergone a renaissance, becoming cleaner, more trendy, and more livable.

Long important to the Native people of the region, Lake Union was known as *XáXu7cHoo,* or "small lake," in Whulshootseed, and *tenas chuck,* or

◀ Bird's-eye view of Lake Union, detail from Augustus Koch drawing, 1891

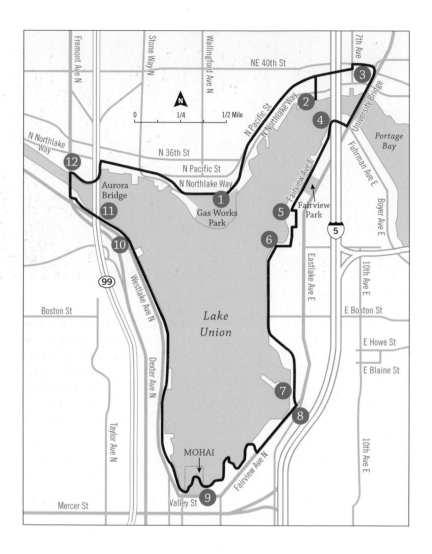

"small water," in Chinook, the local language of trade. The lake earned its current name at Thomas Mercer's 1854 Fourth of July picnic on its shores. Mercer suggested calling the lake "Union," because he thought that someday it would link saltwater and freshwater. (For more information, see Walk 9.)

Looking west over Gas Works Park

With a flat shoreline and a circumference of a little over six miles (excluding Portage Bay), the lake is accessible and easy to circumnavigate on foot. It even has its own signed trail, the Cheshiahud Lake Union Loop, which honors a Duwamish Native who had a home on Portage Bay. This walk focuses primarily on the history of the lake and follows the Cheshiahud Loop. Most of the detail about features occurs during the first four miles, from Gas Works Park to Lake Union Park. The last three miles are more of a stroll.

Start at Gas Works Park. This walk does not explore the park, but you really should do so at some time; it's one of Seattle's most amazing spaces.

❶ As part of his master plan for an integrated park system, landscape architect John Charles Olmsted suggested in 1903 that the city of Seattle should secure this northern end of Lake Union as a park. Three years later, however, the Seattle Lighting Company purchased the land to build a plant for converting coal, and later oil, into synthetic natural gas, or town gas. As with the many other gasification plants around the country, its primary purpose was to produce power for lighting. Unfortunately for anyone who preferred to breathe healthy air, gasification produced toxic fumes and

GAS WORKS PARK

Gas Works Park opened in 1975 after more than a decade of discussions and land purchases. Creating the park was an epic process because few people initially approved of landscape architect Richard Haag's unorthodox vision of marrying the site's gritty industrial story with a more traditional green space. After Haag established an on-site office, opened it to visitors, and began to describe the future park, residents and civic leaders began to realize the potential of his vision.

Perhaps Haag's most radical idea, writes landscape historian Thaisa Way in *The Landscape Architecture of Richard Haag: From Modern Space to Urban Ecological Design*, was to leave the toxic soils in place and treat the material through bioremediation. Workers mixed the soil with sawdust, sewage sludge, leaf litter, and other ingredients, which created an environment for bacteria to help break down the toxins. Haag also formed the most polluted soil and construction waste into the high mound of Kite Hill, which he buried under an 18-inch-thick cap of clay. The steep slopes would lead to water running off and not penetrating into the ground. Nearby valleys and low points further aided bioremediation by altering drainage patterns. Haag's artificial Kite Hill is also an homage to the city's topography, as well as a sly rejoinder to our propensity to regrade said hills.

filthy clouds of smoke, not to mention dangerous by-products such as tar, hydrogen sulfide, and various oils. The Lake Plant closed in 1956 following the introduction of cheaper and cleaner natural gas.

Head north, or clockwise, around the lake on the Burke-Gilman Trail. You might find it less crowded to veer off the trail just north of the park and go up to N Pacific Street. There is a good sidewalk that parallels the trail. Continue about three-quarters of a mile to 4th Avenue NE. Turn right down the steps, continue down the road, and cross NE Northlake Way to Waterway 15, a pocket park on Lake Union.

❷ Designed by Elizabeth Connor, Linda Brodax, and Cliff Wetwerth, this tiny park is one of the more delightful spaces on Lake Union. The artists incorporated used cobblestones and bricks, found objects cast in bronze, and 62 silk-screened images on tile to provide a unique and thoughtful historical timeline of the lake. There is also a hatch cover with a map of the lake. Waterway 15 is one of those spaces where you will want to linger and discover the many charming references to the people and stories of Lake Union, though you may come away with more questions than answers. But that's part of the fun.

> Return to the Burke-Gilman Trail, continue east to 7th Avenue NE, and turn left off the trail to NE 40th Street. Take the upper road with the signs for Cheshiahud Trail and Peace Park. Follow 40th up to the park.

❸ The Burke-Gilman Trail is the former route of the Seattle Lake Shore and Eastern Railway, which Thomas Burke, Daniel Gilman, and others incorporated in 1885. Their goal was to connect Seattle to the eastern part of the state and a transcontinental railroad. By late October 1887, trains were running twice a day from Seattle out to Union Bay.

Floyd Schmoe was a 91-year-old peace activist who led and inspired the efforts to create the Peace Park. After seeing a "Think Globally, Act Locally" bumper sticker in 1986, Schmoe decided to clean up the area that became the park. Two years later, he received the Kiyoshi Tanimoto Peace Award from the Hiroshima Peace Center. He used the funds to help pay for Daryl Smith's bronze statue of Sadako Sasaki, who had died from leukemia 10 years after being exposed to radiation during the Hiroshima bombing. When Sasaki found out she was ill, she attempted to make 1,000 origami paper cranes, as legend held that this would restore her health, but she died before she could reach her goal. Her death inspired thousands to make paper cranes, and the bird became a symbol of peace worldwide. The park was dedicated in 1990. Schmoe lived until 2001.

> Walk south on Eastlake Avenue E across the University Bridge. After crossing the bridge, turn right on Fuhrman Avenue E (follow Cheshiahud signs), and descend under the Interstate 5 bridge to South Passage Point Park.

❹ Originally opened on July 1, 1919, the University Bridge was altered in 1933 with a new grating—steel-mesh instead of creosoted wood—which made the bridge deck less slippery and about half as heavy. This allowed the bridge to be widened to six lanes, with two used for street cars. The new bridge also eliminated the old bridge's wooden support trestles, which regularly had to be replaced because of rot. In the summer of 1930 alone, they caught fire 22 times.

Walk south on Fairview Avenue E to E Hamlin Street. As you walk along Fairview, you will pass by many notable spaces described below. (The numbered
stop corresponds to Hamlin Street.)

❺ Look for pint-size green spaces, which the city designates as Shoreline
Street Ends. In 1996, the City of Seattle passed a resolution to preserve and
enhance access to the 149 street ends that terminate at the water. Despite
what some adjacent landowners may believe, all of these spaces are public,
and anyone should be able to access the water both physically and visually.
Along Fairview, 10 street ends have been developed or are under development.

The first you will find is Good Turn Park, just a short way down Fairview;
don't blink or you could miss it, even at a walking pace. Adjacent landowners Homer Bergren and James Nordstrom decided to turn the overgrown
space into a park in 1993. It was formally dedicated in 2000 and named
after the Boy Scout slogan, "Do a good turn daily."

Just under a quarter of a mile past Good Turn is Fairview Park, another
space recommended for protection as part of Seattle's grand park plan in
the early 1900s but which did not earn that status until the late 1990s. The
adjacent P-Patch was started in 1981 and altered and expanded when Fairview was developed.

Just past the park is a dock with modern houseboats. Ward's Cove, formerly the Seattle headquarters of an Alaska-based fish processing company,
may be the final houseboat development on the lake. Although regulations
and space requirements don't prohibit further development, they do make
the construction of a new area of houseboats challenging enough that more
than a century of new houseboat building on the lake will come to an end.

The earliest Lake Union houseboat dates from 1904, about a decade after
they began appearing on Seattle's other bodies of water. By 1914 there were
several hundred on the lake, often occupied by people in search of cheap
housing. This would be the situation for decades to come. Many wealthier
Seattleites did not necessarily look kindly upon the houseboat crowd and
tried to banish the houseboats several times. Not until the late 1960s did
houseboats start to become more widely accepted and more upscale, in part
because they finally hooked into the city sewer system.

Turn left, walk up Hamlin to the alley (Yale Terrace E), and turn right. Continue
south to E Edgar Street, turn right, or west, walk down a block, and turn left on

Boeing's first plane, the B&W *Bluebill*, Lake Union, 1916

Yale Avonue E. Walk to E Roanoke Street, turn right and walk down to the water and the Roanoke Street Mini Park. If in doubt, look for the Cheshiahud signs.

◯ This handsome little park belies the importance of this location to Lake Union's industrial and residential history. William Boeing built his first airplane here, the B&W *Bluebill*, in a hangar that he owned with Conrad Westerveldt. The first flight of the 125-horsepower biplane took place on June 15, 1916. (A replica is on display at the Museum of Flight; Boeing sold the original to the New Zealand Flying School, where it apparently burned in 1926.) Three years later, Boeing and Eddie Hubbard made the first international delivery of airmail when they flew for three hours from Vancouver, B.C., to Lake Union. By this time, Westerveldt was no longer part of the company, and Boeing had established the headquarters for Boeing Airplane Company along the Duwamish River. The hangar was destroyed in 1971 for a planned-but-never-completed major development, the Roanoke

NEED MONEY FOR A WORLD'S FAIR? SELL LAND

On February 1, 1907, the state legislature passed a bill titled "Providing for the Sale of Certain Shore Lands and Creating Alaska-Yukon-Pacific Exposition Fund." It authorized the state to sell shore lands, primarily around Lake Union, with the goal of raising $1 million to fund the 1909 AYP Exposition, Seattle's first world's fair. The bill's passage had two effects. First, it established the layout and platting of what would become the modern shoreline, including the creation of the 23 water-ways, which are marked out on signs around the lake. Second, it forced those who owned land at the water's edge and who thought they also owned the rights to the water in front of their property to buy the submerged parcels. They had first rights; if they didn't, others could purchase the property.

Reef condominiums. (This name appears on other buildings, none of which were associated with the 1971 proposal.)

Roanoke Reef's developers proposed a 112-unit complex that would have risen 60 feet above the water and extended for a block into the lake. Opposition immediately arose: the Eastlake Community Council and the Floating Homes Association filed lawsuits to stop development. They were later joined by the Washington State Department of Ecology and state Attorney General Slade Gorton. Construction halted in 1974. Many people have argued that this crucial win stopped most further large-scale development along the lake.

Continue south on Fairview Avenue E past E Garfield Street to the Lake Union Drydock Company. Along the way are several spots worth noticing. (The numbered stop corresponds to Drydock.)

❼ The first spot is the Eastlake Bouledrome, where one can play pétanque (pay-*tonk*). Next is the Lynn Street Park, better known as Pete's Park. More information about pétanque and the origin of Pete's Park can be found at each location. Farther down Fairview is Terry Pettus Park, named for the man that Howard Droker, author of *Seattle's Unsinkable Houseboats,* called a "tall, white-bearded prophet." Pettus helped lead the battles against redevelopment plans on the lake in the early 1960s and was instrumental in opposing Roanoke Reef. Just past the park is the former home of the NOAA Pacific Marine Center, which moved to Oregon in 2011.

When you pass E Blaine Street, you will cross into terrain that did not always exist. The original shoreline at Blaine extended almost to Eastlake Avenue E. Over time, fill from a variety of projects, including Interstate 5 and the Battery Street Tunnel, was dumped into Lake Union to make new land. Prior to the addition of fill, trolley companies built trestles to carry their tracks over the water. Only one section of trestle remains; it is visible under the Aurora Bridge (further details below).

Lake Union Drydock Company is the largest remaining connection to the lake's former days as a hub of boat building. Started in 1919 by Otis Cutting and John L McLean, the company was one of many to take advantage of the access to Puget Sound provided by the recently opened ship canal and locks. Cutting and McLean built and repaired boats, eventually employing as many as 300 people by the mid 1920s. Some of their best customers were rumrunners, who needed fast boats to transport booze during Prohibition. Another frequent customer was the Coast Guard, who needed faster boats to catch the bootleggers. At present, Lake Union Drydock focuses on repairing and converting large vessels.

Walk along the water as Fairview Avenue E intersects Fairview Avenue N (coming from the south), and stop near the massive glass dominated building that takes up the east side of the road.

⓪ Now owned by ZymoGenetics, the building is one of two power-generating plants built at Lake Union between 1912 and 1921. The older and smaller one was a hydropower plant that harnessed surplus water flowing downhill from the Volunteer Park reservoir. Though long out of use, the small red tile–roofed building still stands just to the south of the much larger Lake Union Steam Plant. Using oil brought in barges to a dock in Lake Union, the steam plant produced energy via massive boilers. These boilers made steam that ran turbines, which in turn generated electricity. Total capacity was 30,000 kilowatts (an average modern US household uses almost 11,000 kilowatts annually). City Light decommissioned the plant in 1987. ZymoGenetics bought it in 1993 and remodeled and reopened it a year later.

Continue south on Fairview Avenue N to Yale Avenue N. Look for a sign that reads "Cheshiahud Loop, Heels," which points west. Follow that sign and the other Cheshiahud signs, which will take you on a designated path between buildings and the water. If you are in doubt, stay close to the water. The path will eventually take you around to the Center for Wooden Boats and Lake Union Park. (Here you are about halfway around the lake, perhaps a good place to stop for a snack.)

❾ In 1853, David and Louisa Denny were the first to homestead the lake. Thomas Mercer followed soon after and chose property north and west of the Dennys. Little further development occurred at the lake until 1872, when Seattle's first railroad on the lake's southern shore was established. At the time that shore was south of modern-day Mercer Street. To the west, the shoreline was close to 8th Avenue N (then called Vine or Park Street), almost 600 feet from its modern location. The train carried coal that had come from the east side of Lake Washington. From the lake the train traveled one mile to the waterfront at Pike Street. Ten years later, the first mill—Lake Union Lumber and Manufacturing—opened, also on the south shore. From the early 1880s until about 1920, sawmills were the most important industry on the lake. They were supplanted by ship builders after the opening of the ship canal.

In addition to being an economic driver, mills led to landscape change when sawdust and other debris were dumped into the lake to make new land. Other fill material came from various regrade projects, though I have not been able to determine if any came from Denny Hill. By 1912, most of the southern end of the lake had been filled.

Continue around Lake Union on the Cheshiahud Trail until the parking lots end. You are now heading north, through a strange section of trail and parking lots. *Be aware not only of cars but also of bikers and joggers, who often use this route.* This is a long stretch with many shops, a few art projects, and several marinas. There are also several bus stops along Westlake for Metro Route 40, which travels north to Fremont Avenue N and N 34th Street. Consider the following as you stroll along. (The next numbered stop corresponds to the end of the parking lots.)

❿ You are still walking on made land; basically all of Westlake Avenue N and the land east of it did not exist when the Dennys and Mercers homesteaded the area. In 1890, Luther H. Griffith completed an electric railway line, or street car, from the south end of Lake Union to Fremont. Built on

Museum of History and Industry (MOHAI)

THE CENTER FOR WOODEN BOATS, LAKE UNION PARK, AND MOHAI

Since the late 1970s, the Center for Wooden Boats (CWB) has provided a place where people could "learn, build, sail, and play on the water." The hands-on opportunities benefit people of all ages who wish to see the boats, to rent them, and to learn about them.

In 2000, the United States Navy transferred 5 acres to Seattle Parks and Recreation, which increased the total acreage of Lake Union Park to 12. The park's opening ceremony was on September 24, 2010.

The Museum of History and Industry (MOHAI) is one of the great treasures of Seattle. Organized to preserve, interpret, and share Seattle's history, it is well worth a visit. MOHAI first opened on the shore of Union Bay in 1952 and moved to its present location in the former Naval Reserve Building in 2012.

pilings, the railroad went over water on a trestle from about modern-day Westlake and Mercer north around the lake. By 1904, trolley service along the line ran every 12 minutes. It operated until 1940. A year later all of Seattle's electric streetcar trolley service was eliminated, and buses replaced the trolleys.

Trestle of the Seattle Electric Railway and Power Company, west side of Lake Union, Frank La Roche, circa 1891

Perhaps the lake's most curious feature is what happens to it during earthquakes. When seismic waves pass through the ground around Seattle during a quake, they get amplified by the parallel ridges that make up the lake's east and west sides. In the lake, the seismic waves generate water waves known as *seiches*, which can rise up to several feet high. During the 2002 magnitude 7.9 Denali earthquake in Alaska, at least 20 houseboats in the lake were damaged by seiches.

At the end of the parking lots, look for signs for the Cheshiahud Trail, which point you over to Westlake Avenue N. You can take this route, which will lead you to the Fremont Bridge, or you can stay along the water. The advantage of not following the trail is that you can see the final section of train trestle on the lake.

⓫ Just after you pass under the Aurora Bridge, you will reach the last remaining remnants of the former trestle system on the lake. It was built for the Northern Pacific, which also ran north up the west side of Lake Union. Avoid the trestle by walking on the roadway.

If you followed Westlake and the Cheshiahud Trail, continue west to the Fremont Bridge and cross it. If you stayed along the water, look for a stairway to your left just before the Fremont Bridge. Ascend it, turn right, and cross the bridge. Immediately after you cross the bridge, descend the stairs to your right down to the Burke-Gilman Trail. (The numbered stop corresponds to the stairs down to the trail.)

⑫ Completed in June 1917, the Fremont Bridge is the most frequently opened Seattle drawbridge, because it is 12 feet closer to the water than either the Ballard or University Bridges. (Since 1917, the Fremont bridge has opened more often—at least 620,000 times—than any other bridge in the United States.) Developed by Edward C. Kilbourne, Edward and Carrie Blewett, and Luther H. Griffith, the town of Fremont was named in 1888 for the Nebraska hometown of Griffith and the Blewetts. A year later, Corliss P. Stone established Edgewater, which he named for a Chicago lakeside community. To reach Edgewater, people could travel the Seattle Lake Shore and Eastern Railway from downtown Seattle, which stopped at the Edgewater Depot (about due south of the Dump/Transfer Station), or they could catch the steamer *Latona* (owned by the developers) from the south end of Lake Union to a dock near the depot. The third town on the north side of the lake was Latona—described as a "new suburban village"—which James Moore established in late 1889. All three towns were annexed into Seattle in 1891.

Originally located at the north edge of a small town, Lake Union is now in the center of an ever-changing and ever-growing metropolis. But it is more than a geographic quirk on a map: Lake Union has become central to the life of the city. It's where the city congregates to watch the Fourth of July fireworks, where residents and visitors go to learn about the city's history, where kayakers, stand-up paddlers, yacht owners, and everyone in-between comes to enjoy the water, and of course, Lake Union is a place where people live and work. With such a range of dynamic opportunities, it is easy to imagine that the lake will continue to retain its central role in the Seattle story.

Follow the Burke-Gilman Trail east back to Gas Works Park.

The Hiram M. Chittenden Locks and Discovery Park

BOATS, BIRDS, AND BIG TREES

In addition to passing by the locks, wander along one of Seattle's least-known neighborhoods and into Seattle's largest park, Discovery Park.

DISTANCE	4.1 miles
START/END	Hiram M. Chittenden Locks, 3015 NW 54th Street
NOTES	The walk traverses one stretch of hard-packed dirt trail. Discovery Park has public restrooms throughout. There are two relatively steep hills and a three-quarter-mile side trip. August and September are the best times to see migrating salmon here.

The idea of connecting saltwater and freshwater in Seattle was first mentioned publicly at Lake Union in a Fourth of July speech in 1854. Speaking on the lake's shore, pioneer Thomas Mercer suggested the name *Union* be-

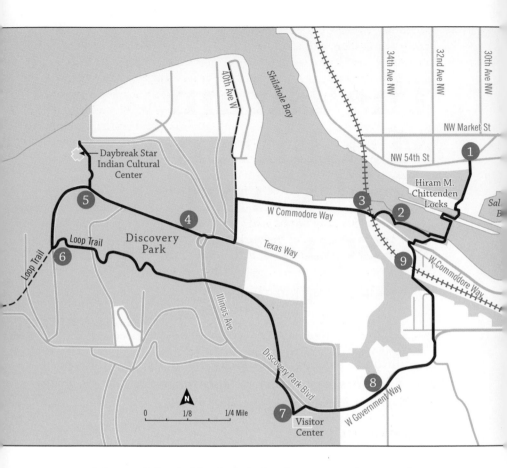

cause of the possibility "of this little body of water sometime providing a connecting link uniting the larger lake [Washington] and Puget Sound." No one, or at least no one with money and manpower, took up the idea until 1883 when landowners around Lake Union and Salmon Bay (the area now behind the locks) hired Chinese labor contractor Wa Chong and others to dig the necessary cuts to link the lakes and connect to Salmon Bay.

Mercer may have been the first settler to suggest linking the lakes, but the Native people had long traveled between freshwater and saltwater; they used canoes and probably portaged overland, exchanging one canoe for another. To them, the area around Salmon Bay was the site of the village known as *sHulsHóól,* or Tucked Away Inside. Another village, *shLoowééhL,* or Little Canoe Channel, was located at what is now the University Village.

Both the federal government and private individuals floated plans to improve on Wa Chong's work, but not until 1911 did construction begin on the present-day locks and ship canal. Five years earlier, Hiram M. Chittenden had arrived in Seattle to head the Army Corps of Engineers's local office. He finally made the project a reality by rallying community support and obtaining federal funding, both of which were necessary to complete the grand scheme.

One of the central challenges of the system was that Lake Washington was 29 feet above sea level, Lake Union was 9 feet lower than Lake Washington, and Salmon Bay was an inlet whose water level fluctuated with the tide. To build only one set of locks, all three bodies of water would have to be brought to the same elevation; the most logical level was that of Lake Union. This choice ultimately required the lowering of the bigger lake and the conversion of Salmon Bay into a lake, or reservoir, 20 feet above sea level.

The gates of the locks closed on July 12, 1916. In August, engineers breached the barrier separating Lake Washington and Lake Union, and for a little over two months water drained until Lake Washington had dropped down to the level of the smaller lake. The official grand opening dedication, carnival, and celebration on July 4, 1917, attracted more than 50,000 people. (The locks were officially named after Chittenden in July 1956.)

Seattleites had several reasons for desiring a canal linking freshwater and saltwater. Primarily, they wanted to create a freshwater port, away from tides, corrosive saltwater, and harmful invertebrates, such as shipworms and gribbles, which could be perniciously devastating to wooden vessels and piers. The city's early citizens also hoped that industries would move in and take advantage of the good connection out to Puget Sound. A further impetus came from the Navy, which had long sought a freshwater base, though by the time the canal opened, there was little demand for a naval facility.

Start at the Hiram M. Chittenden Locks (stop 1 on map). Walk through the main gates (for a good orientation, stop in the visitor center). Proceed into the grounds, and continue across the locks to the fish ladder, long one of the best

Locks under construction, 1914

places in the city to see migrating salmon. The most popular place to watch fish is in the underground viewing area.

❶ At present, a majority of the salmon that migrate through the locks use the ladder, though this varies by species, by year, and by sex: female Chinook apparently prefer the locks. Prior to the 1970s, the ladder was undersized, and most fish probably traveled back into the lake via the locks. A better understanding of how fish migrate led to the changes in ladder design. Peak viewing of Chinook is in late August; Coho peak a month later.

One unanswered question is how the first post-locks salmon found their way back into Lake Washington, since they could no longer access their historic route from Elliott Bay up the Duwamish River to the Black River, the lake's original outlet. One possibility is that some fish had already started using the Salmon Bay to Lake Washington route by traveling up the earlier and much smaller canals. Another is that juvenile fish living in the lake

Heron nest at the rookery at the locks

did not leave the lake until after the locks opened, which meant that the new route was their natural one. And, finally, consider that the distance between the locks and the Duwamish/Black River is miniscule compared to the hundreds to thousands of miles the migrating fish had already traveled; finding the new route may not have posed any problem for the fish. No one collected data at the time to conclusively figure out how the fish did it, so we will never know for sure.

> Walk west, and follow the path along the water. Stop by a small shelter near steps that lead down to the water.

❷ Look up as you walk along. Above you are trees used extensively by cormorants, crows, gulls, and great blue herons (heron nests make up the rookery in the trees). The cormorants are the larger black birds with the hooked bills. This is one of the few spots in Seattle to see the area's three cormorant species—double-crested, pelagic, and Brandt's—the latter two of which are strictly marine species. All three are here for the fish, which they catch by diving into the water and chasing. Or, as poet Robinson Jeffers wrote, cormorants "slip their long black bodies under water and hunt like wolves."

Cormorants are the birds often seen standing with their wings spread in order to dry their feathers. They do so because the birds have what are described as "wettable" feathers. When wet, these feathers collect water and become heavier, a key adaptation for a bird that needs less buoyancy when diving. One final cool word regarding cormorants: *totipalmate*. This describes how webbing joins together all four of the birds' toes. Ducks and gulls have just the front three toes united by webbing.

Keep on the lookout for seals and bald eagles, both of which take advantage of the salmon that move through the locks.

> The path soon curves up to W Commodore Way. Turn right, and walk west until you are under the train tracks across Shilshole Bay.

❸ The Great Northern Railroad built Bridge No. 4 in 1914. It is a bascule bridge, or drawbridge, which operates by a counterweight (500 tons of concrete) that balances the span. Trains traveling north out of Seattle initially crossed Salmon Bay on wooden trestles at 14th Avenue W (a little over a mile to the east), but the train routes had to be moved in preparation for the opening of the locks.

As you pass under the train tracks, look to the right for a pole, topped by a nest on a wooden platform. The nest platform was built in 2011 for osprey, another bird that exploits the abundance of fish in the water around the locks. Osprey (whether the same pair or not is unknown) have used the nest and fledged several young since construction of the platform, though bald eagles have also besieged the osprey and driven them away during the nesting season.

> Continue west on W Commodore Way to 40th Avenue W. If you want to see an unusual view of Seattle, turn right on 40th, and walk just over one-third mile out 40th, which ends at a small public green space overlooking Shilshole Bay. (The green space may look private but it isn't.)
>
> If you prefer not to make this detour, turn left at 40th and walk up to where the road T's at Texas Way. Turn right, walk into Discovery Park, and continue west on a path that runs along the parking lot. Stop at a very short path on the right, which leads to an overlook of a series of cascades.

❹ Discovery Park became city property in 1973. Formerly, the land had been part of Fort Lawton, an Army post named in 1900 for General Henry Ware Lawton, best known for capturing Geronimo. During World War II, more than 1,100 German prisoners of war were housed at the base. By the 1960s, Fort Lawton was little used and a citizen group formed with the goal of converting the land to park property. With the help of Senator Henry M. Jackson, legislation eventually was passed that facilitated the acquisition of the old fort property.

Over the years, numerous projects have been established to restore the land to more natural conditions. In 2012 a restoration effort occurred during a larger project to fix a waterline under the parking lot that you have been walking along. The Seattle Parks Department and several community partners daylighted a small creek that had previously flowed in a pipe. Among the project's novel aspects was directing the stream into an artificial series of drops, or cascades, which allows the water to descend a steep slope without causing erosion. To keep the cost low and also create a functional and aesthetic look, designers made each cascade out of a precast manhole base. The creek is known as Scheuerman Creek for Christian Scheuerman, who homesteaded 160 acres in the Interbay area. *Please do not attempt to walk down the slope as this will harm plants and cause erosion.*

> At the end of the parking lot, continue along the pavement, and look for a smallish sign pointing to Daybreak Star Indian Cultural Center. The route leads to a larger sign indicating the building. To explore Daybreak and get a great view, turn off to the right. The walk continues on from this larger sign.

❺ Daybreak Star opened in 1977 and is the home of the United Indians of All Tribes (UIAT) Foundation. In 1970, about one hundred Native Americans and their supporters occupied the Fort Lawton military base, which the federal government had decided to relinquish after 72 years of ownership. The protestors had come to claim the land for Native Americans who lived in and around Seattle. After many months of protests and negotiations, UIAT eventually acquired 16 acres of land and built Daybreak Star as an urban base, providing social and cultural services to Seattle's Native community. It is open to the public on weekdays and is home to an art gallery. North of the building is a stunning overlook out to Puget Sound.

Back at the main route, follow the road as it ascends toward the forested part of Discovery Park. Continue about one-quarter mile until you intersect a trail crossing the road. Turn left, or east, and follow the Loop Trail into the forest. Stop at any point, or continue on, crossing two roads and eventually passing by a huge, multi-trunked tree on the right side of the trail. (The numbered stop corresponds to the left turn onto the Loop Trail.)

❻ The trail passes through lovely groves of bigleaf maples, one of the more widespread and abundant native trees in the city. Often found with another native tree, red alder (characterized by its gray, birch-like bark and oval leaves with toothed margins), on disturbed ground such as landslides, bigleaf maples thrive best in moist woods. Some develop massive trunks and grow to heights of well over 100 feet tall. Bigleaf maples were widely planted as a street tree in Seattle, though this practice was banned in 1961 because of the trees' tendency to break up sidewalks and streets with their large trunks and roots.

As the name suggests, the bigleaf maple leaves are huge, typically up to 12 inches wide but occasionally up to 24 inches. The leaves can turn a brilliant yellow in fall, which complements the mosses, ferns, and lichens that adorn trunks and branches. Large bigleaf maples may support up to a ton of mosses. In the park, perhaps the maples' most noticeable epiphytes are licorice ferns, which were eaten by various Native tribes and used for colds and sore throats.

Follow the Loop Trail to the visitor center.

❼ The visitor center has restrooms and good information about the park's natural and human history.

From the visitor center, return back toward the Loop Trail and veer right to a paved path along the park's main road. Walk out of the park, and continue east on the north side of W Government Way to just past 35th Avenue W and the Kiwanis Ravine.

❽ The Kiwanis Club of Seattle donated the ravine to the city in 1956. Decades of dumping yard waste and less benign materials led in 1984 to a group forming to protect the wooded landscape. In 2010, the city designated the ravine as Seattle's first wildlife sanctuary, in part because it had become home to Seattle's largest great blue heron colony. About 90 nests

A massive bigleaf maple

dotted the trees by 2013, though most of the birds abandoned the nests and built new ones in Commodore Park in 2014, probably due to bald eagle harassment.

Continue east on W Government Way to 32nd Avenue W. Turn left and follow 32nd as it veers north. When the sidewalk terminates at the end of the block, be careful: you will proceed by walking in the relatively quiet street. As 32nd curves to the left, look for a path leading off to the right and to a surprising pedestrian bridge. Watch for bikes—the path is a popular bike route.

❾ The Great Northern Railroad built this pedestrian bridge in 1914 to provide the westernmost route over what were then new train tracks across Shilshole Bay. Except for minor repairs, the bridge consists of most of its original wood. Considering how few people lived at the north end of Magnolia, it is not clear why the city required Great Northern to build the bridge. Some residents probably took the bridge to get to jobs at Ballard's shipping and lumber businesses, but perhaps the bridge also served the soldiers at Fort Lawton, who may have taken advantage of it and the locks for a quick route to certain pleasures in Ballard.

The bridge ends at 33rd Avenue W, which continues down to W Commodore Way. Cross the street, and follow the path that leads back to the locks and your starting point.

As you return to the beginning of the walk, observe who uses the locks. I suspect that the early ship canal advocates could not imagine what has happened with Lake Washington, the locks, and Lake Union. Only a small amount of industry has taken over the shorelines of the lake. The dreams of a freshwater port never materialized, and no Navy fleets dock in the restorative freshwater. (To see a remnant of the military connection, look west from the locks and note that you cannot see Puget Sound. Chittenden and others considered the locks a potential target for "hostile attack in time of war" and located it to take advantage of natural cover.) The most common users of the locks are pleasure crafts, which outnumber commercial vessels more than four to one.

Thomas Mercer was correct that a connection between Lake Washington and Puget Sound through *his* Lake Union would help transform Seattle, but like other cities, Seattle has evolved and changed from the vision of its earliest settlers. Today people now choose to live in Seattle not just for jobs but also because they can easily access the beauty of its natural areas. Likewise, they value its residents' commitment to protecting and enhancing the lives of the other species that inhabit the area. Few places in the city exemplify this change better than the locks.

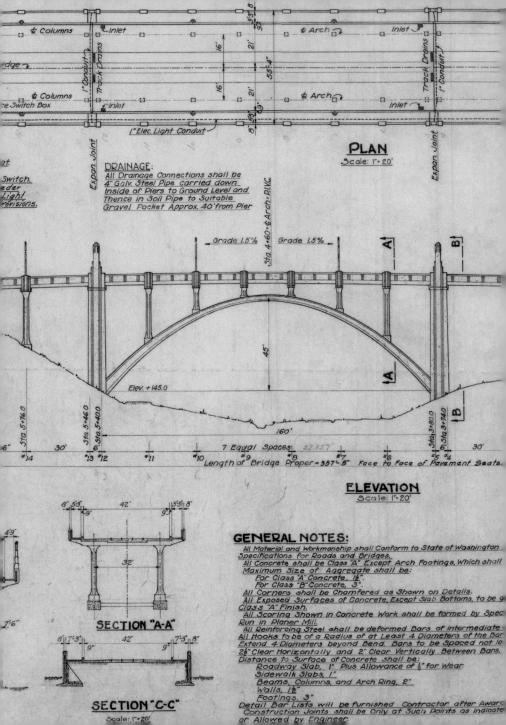

PLAN
Scale: 1" = 20'

DRAINAGE:
All Drainage Connections shall be 4" Galv. Steel Pipe carried down Inside of Piers to Ground Level and Thence in Soil Pipe to Suitable Gravel Pocket Approx. 40' from Pier

Grade 1.5%   Grade 1.5%

Sta. 4+60 - ℄ Arch - R.W.C.

45'

Elev. +145.0

160'

7 Equal Spaces = 22.857'
Length of Bridge Proper = 357'-5"   Face to Face of Pavement Seats.

ELEVATION
Scale: 1" = 20'

SECTION "A-A"

42'   32'

SECTION "C-C"
Scale: 1" = 20'

42'

GENERAL NOTES:
All Material and Workmanship shall Conform to State of Washington Specifications for Roads and Bridges.
All Concrete shall be Class "A" Except Arch Footings, Which shall
Maximum Size of Aggregate shall be:
  For Class "A" Concrete, 1½".
  For Class "B" Concrete, 3".
All Corners shall be Chamfered as Shown on Details.
All Exposed Surfaces of Concrete, Except Slab Bottoms, to be a Class "A" Finish.
All Scoring Shown in Concrete Work shall be formed by Special Run in Planer Mill.
All Reinforcing Steel shall be deformed Bars of Intermediate
All Hooks to be of a Radius of at Least 4 Diameters of the Bar Extend 4 Diameters beyond Bend. Bars to be Spaced not le 2½" Clear Horizontally and 2" Clear Vertically Between Bars.
Distance to Surface of Concrete shall be:
  Roadway Slab, 1" Plus Allowance of ½" for Wear.
  Sidewalk Slabs, 1".
  Beams, Columns, and Arch Ring, 2".
  Walls, 1½".
  Footings, 3".
Detail Bar Lists will be furnished Contractor after Award
Construction Joints shall be Only at Such Points as indicate
or Allowed by Engineer.

Green Lake to Lake Washington

TRACING A HISTORIC CREEK

This somewhat strenuous trek along streets, parks, and the Burke-Gilman Trail follows the original drainage of Ravenna Creek.

DISTANCE	4.7 miles
STARTING POINT	East side of Green Lake, near community center/Evans Pool
ENDING POINT	Union Bay Natural Area, 3501 NE 41St Street
NOTES	The last half mile leads to Metro Bus route 45, which returns to the starting point. About halfway through the walk, there is an opportunity to return to Green Lake, and make this a roundtrip. There are a couple short sections of gravel path. Restrooms can be found at the University Village and at the Center for Urban Horticulture.

For thousands of years, Green Lake and Lake Washington were connected by Ravenna Creek, which flowed southeast down what is now Ravenna Boulevard before veering slightly north and continuing through the densely forested ravine of what became Ravenna Park. The creek emerged from the

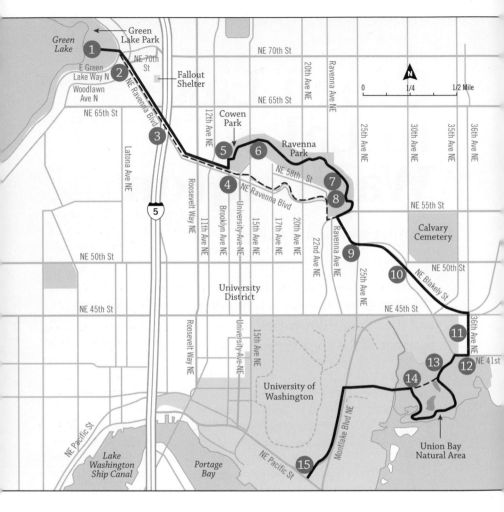

ravine and into a sphagnum bog that spread across the area now covered by University Village. Its journey ended in Lake Washington at Union Bay, which historically extended north to modern NE 45th Street, about one-half mile north of today's shoreline.

Ravenna Creek vanished from its upper reach when workers put the water into a pipe as part of the North Trunk Sewer system. Built because of concerns over typhoid and cholera in contaminated drinking water, the North Trunk consolidated outflow north of the soon-to-be-built Lake Washington Ship Canal via 22 miles of sewer pipes, the largest of which had a 12-foot diameter. The system extended from West Point on Magnolia to Green Lake, with the Ravenna pipe section completed in 1911. Following the elimination of the creek, the city opened the 160-foot-wide Ravenna Boulevard, which included a bridle path, planting strip, and roadways. In 1961, the city replaced the original paths with grass.

This one-way walk traces the historic route of Ravenna Creek and explores the many changes along the drainage including the lowering of Lake Washington and drying out of the bog, the felling of the massive trees in Ravenna Park, and the filling in of part of Cowen Park with dirt and debris from the construction of Interstate 5. This is one of the more difficult walks in the book, in part because it goes on gravel paths through Ravenna and Cowen Parks and the Union Bay Natural Area, so you will need to pay a bit more attention to route-finding than on other walks.

Start on the eastern shore of Green Lake between the community center and ball field.

❶ Green Lake originally covered what are now the park's ball fields and the community center and its parking lot. A General Land Office survey around the lake found a forest of Douglas fir (eight feet in diameter), west ern red cedar, western hemlock, red alder, and maples, both vine (closer to the creek) and bigleaf. Along the lakeshore were dense, brushy areas of salmonberry and willow.

The fertile land attracted settlers and developers, including Guy Phinney, who built a small mill at the lake that could cut 10,000 board feet a day. Although the land was far from the center of population in Seattle, a trolley connected Green Lake to downtown. The tracks initially ran along the east side of the lake and around to the north end but ultimately completed a loop around the lake and back down the west side.

Three years after Ravenna Creek disappeared into its pipe, the city, on the advice of park designer John Charles Olmsted (of the Olmsted Broth ers firm), lowered the lake seven feet, which added 100 acres of new land to the park, primarily around the lake's outlet. By this time, most of the lake had been logged, streets had been platted, and numerous houses had been built.

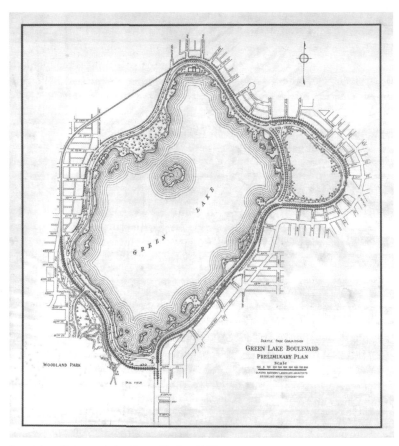

Green Lake preliminary park plan, Olmsted Brothers, 1910

Walk east from the lake on the paved path between the community center and the ball fields. Cross E Green Lake Way N so that you are on the north side of NE Ravenna Boulevard, next to Gregg's Cycles. Walk east on Ravenna, and cross the odd three-way intersection of NE 70th Street, Woodlawn Avenue N, and Ravenna to the east side and in front of a triangular building topped by a clock. Look near that building's front door for a map of Green Lake in the pavement.

❷ Artist Carolyn Law created this map of the lake in 2010. The green terrazzo marks the modern lake edge, and the line surrounding it indicates the historic shoreline. The largest of the buildings on the lake's edge is the community center, with the wedge-shaped Aqua Theater closest to Ravenna Boulevard and the sort of ear-shaped wading pool at the lake's north end. Law hoped that as this neighborhood developed and people had to slow down for increased traffic, they would pay attention and notice the details of the lake.

> Continue east on Ravenna Boulevard until you are under Interstate 5. As you walk along, note the large caiman sculpture filled with plants on the lawn in front of the John Marshall School. Observe also the tall trees growing along the boulevard. These include English oaks, sycamore maples, and red maples, none of which are native. Also, if you do the walk when the trees have no leaves, look for the many squirrel nests, which look like balls of clumped leaves.

❸ Artist Sheila Klein completed her art piece *Columnseum* in 2007 by painting more than 250 columns in the 10 acre space under I-5. Klein's website notes that "rather than fight the massive existing infrastructure, the project works with the site's own visual vocabulary: parking paint and concrete columns. The lot was painted with simple shapes drawn from parking lot vernacular (white stripes/blue handicap) to minimize the dark space and accentuate the architecture."

Plans for a freeway linking Seattle to Tacoma and Everett started in the early 1950s but did not gain full momentum until the passage of the Na-

THE COLD WAR IN SEATTLE

Perhaps the most unusual structure associated with I-5 is a nuclear fallout shelter built under the freeway on Weedin Place (across from 68th Avenue NE), just north of the north end of the Ravenna Park and Ride. Designed to house 200 people for two weeks, the shelter had diesel-powered electricity generators, an air circulation system, a well, and piping connected to the city's water and sewer systems. Fortunately, no one needed to use the space for its intended purpose, and it ended up serving more prosaic functions as a storage facility and a driver's license bureau for the Washington Department of Transportation. (Only the front door is visible at the site.)

tional Interstate and Defense Highways Act of 1956. Early sections of what became Interstate 5 opened in 1962 with the complete route from Everett to Tacoma opening five years later.

Continue east on Ravenna Boulevard to Brooklyn Avenue NE.

❹ At this point, the subterranean, six-foot-diameter North Trunk Sewer pipe carrying Ravenna Creek continues southeast under the ridge that begins to rise to the east and descends to a connector near what is now University Village. Contractors initially attempted to dig the pipe's underground route through the 17th Avenue ridge with a boring machine, which worked on roughly the same principle as its much larger, modern descendant, Bertha. However, this first-ever attempt at tunnel boring in Seattle failed because of mechanical problems. The contractor then came up with the novel solution of digging the tunnel by hand with picks and shovels and lining it with brick. Workers advanced through the ridge averaging about 50 feet per week.

Turn left and enter Cowen Park at NE 61st Street.

❺ Real estate developer Charles Cowen donated 12 acres of land to the city for this park in 1906. He is honored by a sign on the park's gates at University Way NE. Originally dominated by a ravine with a meandering Ravenna Creek, the park changed substantially in 1960 with the addition of 100,000 cubic yards of fill from the construction of I-5. Although many neighbors approved of eliminating the ravine, which they thought was the "biggest nest for juvenile delinquency in the city," others called the filling of the ravine "outrageous."

Follow the dirt and gravel path in Cowen Park that curves left, or north, down and into the Ravenna Park ravine until you are under the high concrete bridge. (Numerous signed trails run through the park. This route takes you along the main trail in the bottom of the ravine.)

❻ A two-level wooden pedestrian bridge formerly crossed the Ravenna ravine at 15th Avenue NE. The bridge above you, which marks the boundary between Cowen and Ravenna Parks, was built as a Works Progress Administration project in 1936 and reflects the Art Deco aesthetic of the era. The apex of the graceful arch is 60 feet above the creek. Farther east is the 20th Avenue Bridge, built in 1913–14 for about $55,000. It was closed to motor vehicles in 1975 after engineers determined it needed costly upgrades for continued automobile traffic. Both bridges are city landmarks.

Ravenna Creek follows a route that is a bit anomalous in Seattle. The city's predominant topographic features are north–south trending ridges and troughs that developed during the last ice age. (For more information, see Walk 12.) In contrast, Ravenna Creek and the nearby Lake Washington Ship Canal cut against the grain in northwest–southeast trending channels. Geologists propose that the waterways follow topographic lows that developed under the ice and were then enlarged by water at the base of the glacier. Why the channels trend the way they do is less clear. They could mirror either an unrecognized tectonic structure or a deeply buried structure in the bedrock, but there is no undisputed evidence for either structure. No matter what caused the ravine that Ravenna Creek follows through Ravenna Park, it formed one of the great geological curiosities of our local topography.

Although the upper part of Ravenna Creek is locked into a sewer pipe, numerous seeps, springs, and small tributaries provide enough water for the creek to flow year round in Cowen and Ravenna Parks.

Continue along about half a mile until you cross over the creek to an open space with a bench and concrete slab.

❼ In 1887, Reverend William W. and Louise Beck purchased 400 acres near Union Bay, including the property that the previous owners George and Oltilde Dorffel had named Ravenna Spring Park after Ravenna, Italy. (The great Romantic poet Lord Byron wrote of "Ravenna's immemorial wood.") On part of their new land, the Becks established the town of Ravenna, which later had a post office, grist mill, and Seattle Female College. The City of Seattle annexed Ravenna in 1907.

The Becks fenced off part of the ravine and charged visitors 25 cents to enter. Attractions included a sulfur spring cleverly named the "Wood Nymphs Well"; "Ye Merrie Makers' Inn," a 40-by-90-foot pavilion; and several picnic shelters and wading ponds. The small concrete cistern-like structure surrounded by flagstones near the creek is the location of the sulfur spring. A public works project during the Depression sealed off the spring because of concern that it was a public health hazard.

But the biggest attractions, literally and figuratively, were the towering Douglas firs, or what some referred to as "vegetable skyscrapers." To attract attention to the trees, the Becks named several of the biggest, honoring people such as pianist Jan Paderewski (Louise Beck taught piano), Theodore Roosevelt, and Robert E. Lee. Apparently the Becks also felt that a little hyperbole would help: they claimed that the Lee tree topped out at more than 400 feet. But it couldn't have reached quite so high—no Douglas fir that tall has ever been found. More believable is that one tree had a circumference of 44 feet, though the Becks measured it closer to the ground than modern tree-circumference fanatics would. But these great trees did not survive long into the 20th century.

In 1910, the city acquired the park through condemnation proceedings from the Becks for $144,920. Within a few years, the Parks Department had cut down the Roosevelt tree, noting that it was a "threat to public safety." Hugo Winkenwerder, dean of the University of Washington's College of Forestry, declared the trees healthy and not in need of any additional assistance from the Parks Department, but more cutting ensued despite assurances from Parks Superintendent J. W. Thompson. People cited car pollution, storms, and chimney smoke as justification for the removal of the trees. Seattle Parks Department historian Don Sherwood, however, noted that unjustified tree cutting regularly occurred in the parks. "Just label it 'diseased' and out it went," he said. All of the big trees were gone by the end of the 1920s, and no physical evidence of them, such as stumps, remains.

Continue along the creek (don't ascend out of the ravine) until wooden fences are on both sides of the path.

❽ More enlightened stewardship has dominated Ravenna Park in the past few decades, particularly along the bottomland of the ravine where University of Washington students, private citizens, and groups such as Earth-Corps have restored habitat. This has included removing invasive plant species, planting native ones, and mulching. Small flags often indicate on-going restoration sites. *Do not disturb them.*

Arguably the most dramatic restoration occurred along the lower reach of the creek. More than a decade of debate and planning between the city, county, and citizen groups such as the Ravenna Creek Alliance led in 2006 to daylighting Ravenna Creek and restoring it to more than 650 feet of its historic route through Ravenna Park. No longer would the creek drop into a sewer pipe and disappear underground. Now it flows aboveground, providing habitat for a wealth of plants and animals. The restored creek starts approximately where you stand.

> Continue along the path and around the left side of the ball field, past the drain where Ravenna Creek returns to a pipe, which carries the water to Union Bay. When you reach a flight of steps, ascend them. (If you want to return to Green Lake here, via a slightly different route, check the map for a red-dotted line that will guide you back to the starting point. This shorter roundtrip walk is 3.7 miles.) Turn right at the top of the steps, walk to Ravenna Place NE, and turn left, or south, on Ravenna Place. Follow Ravenna until it intersects NE Blakeley Street. You are now on the Burke-Gilman Trail.

❾ On April 15, 1885, Thomas Burke and Daniel Gilman led a group of Seattle investors in forming the Seattle Lake Shore and Eastern (SLS&E) Railway Company, with plans to cross the Cascade Mountains to eastern Washington. Heading north out of downtown, the tracks went through Smith Cove (present-day Interbay), past Salmon Bay, and around the north ends of Lake Union and Lake Washington. Burke and Gilman chose this route for several reasons: the route south out of Seattle was taken by another railroad company, and the two hoped to connect their route to a spur of the transcontinental rail.

Workers laid the SLS&E tracks in nine months to the town of Yesler, about a half mile farther east from where you stand. The roundtrip from downtown to Yesler took 90 minutes. The tracks eventually extended to present-day Bothell and farther. Trains used the tracks on a regular basis until 1963. In 1971, Burlington Northern (a later manifestation of the Northern Pacific Railroad, which had acquired the SLS&E in 1901) abandoned the line. Pushed by citizen activists, the city acquired the rights to the train tracks and opened the first section of the Burke-Gilman Trail in 1974. Four years later the full route from Kenmore to Gas Works Park was completed.

> Cross 25th Avenue NE, and continue east on the Burke-Gilman Trail to 30th Avenue NE.

❿ Historically, a spur line of the SLS&E veered off the main route at this point to the small town of Yesler. The railroad made this large curve around what is now University Village because, prior to 1916, the lowland was a sphagnum bog. Like most local bogs, the Ravenna bog was a complex landscape of open water, floating mats of decomposing plants, and an overstory of shrubs. After the construction of the Lake Washington Ship Canal and the lowering of Lake Washington by nine feet, the bog began to dry out. (For more information, see Walk 9.) University Village opened on the former bog in 1954.

Continue east on the trail across a wooden bridge over a small valley and around a curve to a flight of stairs at 36th Avenue NE. Descend the stairs, cross NE 45th Street, and continue south on 36th Avenue NE to NE 43rd Street.

⓫ You are now in the heart of Yesler. If you had been walking down this road in the 1890s, you would have been on Thornell Street, named for William Thornell, former general manager of the SLS&E and the man who helped bring Seattle's first professional baseball team to town. In 1888, Henry Yesler platted his eponymous town on 23 acres of land he had purchased from Joe Surber. Surber had homesteaded 165 acres in 1872, mostly east of here, and is infamous for killing what some claim was the last cougar in Seattle in 1895. Yesler is best known for the first sawmill on Elliott Bay, which became Seattle's first important business in 1852.

As Seattle grew and logging spread farther from the original town center, Henry Yesler decided to build a new mill on the shore of Lake Washington to more easily exploit forests around the lake. The town of Yesler, which housed sawmill employees, had a one-room schoolhouse, two churches, and a post office. (The postmaster trained his dog to run to the railroad tracks and fetch mail tossed from the SLS&E train.) The mill eventually employed 36 men, who could cut up to 75,000 board feet of lumber every 12 hours. The City of Seattle annexed Yesler in 1907. None of the town of Yesler's nonresidential buildings remain.

Continue south on 36th Avenue NE and cross NE 41st Street to the south side, adjacent to the Center for Urban Horticulture (CUH).

⓬ Established in 1984, CUH is part of the University of Washington Arboretum. The center includes a library, demonstration gardens, classrooms, research facilities, and the Union Bay Natural Area (UBNA; open daily).

Turn right, or west, and walk to the end of the CUH building and a paved path that veers off to the left. Take the path, and cross the small road onto a dirt path, labeled Wahkiakum Lane. Follow the path to a kiosk, where there is good

Feeding frenzy at the Montlake Fill, 1954

information on paths, birds, and flowers. The Natural Area, about 74 acres of wetland, pond, and shoreline, is unofficially known as the Montlake Fill.

⑬ Before 1916, Union Bay was open water that extended north to NE 45th Street and from the base of Laurelhurst across to modern-day Montlake Boulevard. With the post-canal lower lake level, the bay became a cattail marsh. In 1926 the city began dumping trash in the marsh's northeast corner. The marsh eventually became one of Seattle's primary dumps, where up to 110 truckloads of garbage arrived every day. Crews burned the industrial and household materials in open fires, but after complaints from neighbors, they began covering the trash with soil in the 1950s. By 1966, when the dump closed, 200 acres of marsh had been filled with trash and dirt, all of which now lies under parking lots, a driving range, storage yards, playfields, CUH, and UBNA.

Large-scale organized restoration of UBNA didn't start until 1990. By this time, invasive plants such as Scot's broom, purple loosestrife, and

Bufflehead

Himalayan blackberry covered the former dump, although native red alder and black cottonwood had colonized wetter areas. Crews began by removing purple loosestrife, followed by blackberry. These removal efforts continue to the present. The University of Washington, which owns the site, has more than 35 restoration projects focused on removing invasives, adding native plants, and increasing biodiversity and habitat diversity.

To provide access to visitors, researchers, and students, a little more than a mile of hard-packed, handicap accessible trail winds through the restored landscape. Birders have reported seeing more than 250 bird species, including Cooper's hawks, ruddy ducks, barn owls, pileated woodpeckers, song sparrows, and buffleheads. Other inhabitants include coyotes, salamanders, dragonflies, butterflies, and turtles.

Like so many other creeks in Seattle, Ravenna and its outlet are not as diverse as they once were. But the many restoration projects have given these places a new life and new lives. They are ecosystems where visitors have the magical opportunity to encounter the natural world: the beauty of bigleaf maples erupting with golden fall foliage, the stoop of a hungry bald eagle over an unsuspecting duck, the slow deliquescing of mushrooms, or the first rays of the sun on a dewy patch of sedges. As can be seen at UBNA and along Ravenna Creek, restoration is not simply about habitat: it's also about creating opportunity for plants and animals (including humans).

Follow the main path into UBNA, and take the second left, designated as the Loop Trail on the UBNA's map on the kiosk, and follow it around the shoreline. This route offers fine birding and great views out over the lake and, if it's clear, down to Mount Rainier. Stop when you find a nice place to look out over the lake. Wherever you stop would have been underwater prior to 1916.

⑭ You have completed all of the walk except for the section to the Metro Bus route 45. The following directions take you to the bus stop (15 on map).

Continue around the Loop Trail to where it joins the main path (Wahkiakum Lane on UBNA map), and follow it past a wetlands on your left to a bridge that spans a narrow waterway. Cross the bridge, and continue west to a paved walkway heading west between the UW soccer field and the UW outdoor track. The walkway ends at a parking lot. Continue west across the lot (*be careful—watch for traffic*) to a pedestrian overpass on the far side (look for the two sets of stairs that lead to the overpass). Take the overpass over Montlake Boulevard NE to the Burke-Gilman Trail, turn left, and follow the trail about half a mile. About a hundred feet before you go under a large overpass, turn right off the Burke-Gilman to a paved side trail that leads to the overpass, which leads to the light-rail station. Cross the overpass over the Burke-Gilman to a broad open space. Veer right to the southwest and look for a paved path leading to NE Pacific Street, the large road between you and the University of Washington Medical Complex buildings to the south. Follow the path to a flight of stairs down to the stop for Metro Bus route 45 on Pacific. Take the bus west back to Green Lake.

Meadowbrook Pond and Thornton Creek

RESTORATION AND RENEWAL

This short walk focuses on ecosystem restoration in Seattle's largest watershed.

DISTANCE	2.7 miles
START/END	Meadowbrook Community Center, just north of NE 105th Street and west of 35th Avenue NE
NOTES	Restrooms are available at the beginning at the community center. This walk offers an optional side trip that explores a lush, undeveloped park space that requires a bit of route finding. Do not let your dog in the creek as the water contains hazardous substances.

Thornton Creek has the largest watershed of any creek in Seattle with a total drainage of 7,400 acres (about seven percent of the 84-square-mile city). The creek consists of two branches that unite just above Meadowbrook Pond. The north fork flows out of Ronald Bog (N 175th Street and Meridian Avenue N) to Twin Ponds (N 155th Street and Corliss Avenue N) and then under Interstate 5 and through Jackson Park Golf Course before cutting southeast toward the confluence. The south fork starts near North

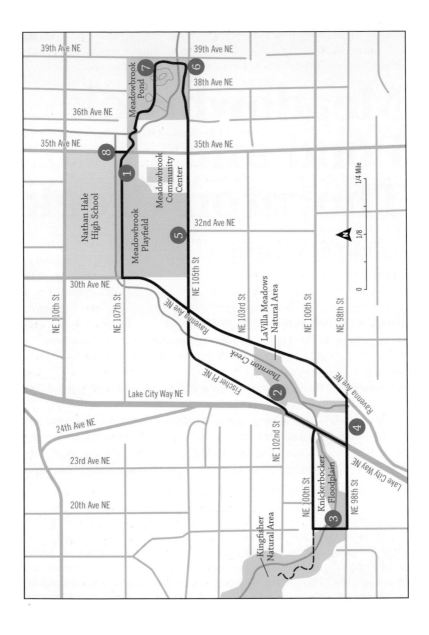

39th Ave NE

Meadowbrook Pond

(7)

(6)

39th Ave NE

38th Ave NE

36th Ave NE

35th Ave NE

(8)

35th Ave NE

(1)

Nathan Hale High School

Meadowbrook Community Center

Meadowbrook Playfield

32nd Ave NE

(5)

30th Ave NE

NE 110th St

NE 107th St

Ravenna Ave NE

NE 105th St

NE 103rd St

LaVilla Meadows Natural Area

NE 100th St

NE 98th St

Thornton Creek

24th Ave NE

Fischer Pl NE

Lake City Way NE

(2)

Ravenna Ave NE

(4)

23rd Ave NE

NE 102nd St

20th Ave NE

Kingfisher Natural Area

NE 100th St

Knickerbocker Floodplain

NE 98th St

Lake City Way NE

(3)

1/4 Mile

1/8

0

Seattle College, flows south of Northgate Mall, where a large bog used to be, and zigzags east through three small parks and under several large roads to meet the north fork at Meadowbrook Pond. The united Thornton Creek continues southeast through numerous yards and enters Lake Washington at Matthews Beach Park.

As happened with the city's other creeks, Thornton has been transformed over the past 150 years from a salmon-filled waterway flowing freely through dense forest into an often channelized, mostly salmon-free creek surrounded by concrete. The modern terrain of impervious surfaces, which covers over 50 percent of the watershed, has rendered the creek invisible to most of the watershed's inhabitants, half of whom couldn't name Thornton or its tributaries when asked in a 1998 poll to identify a creek near their home.

And yet Thornton Creek has received as much attention as any stream in the city and could easily be a poster child for the best and worst ways that we treat streams in the urban landscape. On the plus side, Thornton flows aboveground for over 90 percent of its route through several mostly undeveloped parks. It is also a creek on which public agencies, nonprofit organizations, and neighbors have spent tens of millions of dollars and contributed uncounted hours to restoring and protecting the waterway. On the negative side, the creek regularly floods and fecal coliform levels consistently exceed Washington state safety criteria, while stream sediments contain pesticides, heavy metals, PCBs, and hydrocarbons detrimental to aquatic life.

This walk focuses on the lower end of the south fork of Thornton. It begins along some of the lowest-quality habitat in the fork and ends along some of the best habitat, all of which has been completely altered by people.

> Start at the north end of the parking lot for the Meadowbrook Community Center. From the northwest corner, follow the paved trail that leads through the trees and eventually to another parking lot. Thornton Creek runs along the north side of the pavement. To the south is the Meadowbrook Playfield. Stop along the creek next to the parking lot.

❶ August and Wilhelmine Fischer, German immigrants who arrived in Seattle in 1888, initially owned most of the land near what is now Meadowbrook Playfield. (Quite a few German immigrants moved to this area, which became known as German Hill.) Because of seeps and springs on the hill, the land was constantly soggy and unsuitable for homes but not for activities where land stability was less important. In 1931, Time Oil Company developed the nine-hole Meadowbrook Golf Course, which remained open until 1960 when Seattle Public Schools acquired the land to build a high school. It was going to be called Meadowbrook until a policy change resulted in it being named after Nathan Hale, a hero of the Revolutionary War.

This is the final stretch of the south fork of Thornton Creek. Despite some efforts to improve the waterway, the straightened route along the high school is far from ideal, as the narrow creek flows faster than it would if it could meander, and it has no room to spread out when flooding. These characteristics translate to more erosion and greater transportation of sediments downstream. More sediment is a problem because it can harm salmon habitat and end up in people's homes during flooding. In addition, the channelized creek provides little good habitat, such as pools and protective wood debris, for salmon. Later in the walk are several places where restoration projects have attempted to create conditions more favorable to fish and people.

Walk west through the parking lot to 30th Avenue NE (which soon becomes Ravenna Avenue NE), turn left, or south, and continue walking until NE 105th Street (which becomes Fischer Place NE). Turn right. You will soon cross over Thornton Creek at 27th Avenue NE. Stop, look into the creek, and note the attempts to improve fish habitat, such as the addition of large woody debris and the creation of pools. Continue south on Fischer to a brick building with a sign that reads LaVilla Dairy. *Be careful of traffic as there is no sidewalk.*

❷ In 1922, the Fischers platted the Highway Garden Tracts adjacent to what was then Victory Boulevard (now Lake City Way) and Pacific Highway (now Ravenna Avenue NE). Three years earlier, their daughter Anna had married Norwegian native Ole R. Blindheim, who built the LaVilla Dairy on land donated by his in-laws. Blindheim had previously farmed cows but after several were run over by trains (near the present-day Burke-Gilman Trail) and others were destroyed because of tuberculosis, he started a pasteurization plant to deliver safer milk. In 1993, Ole's son Alvin sold the property behind the building along Thornton Creek to the city so that the land and waterway would remain intact and undeveloped. It is now known as the LaVilla Meadows Natural Area. You are welcome to visit it; the access

LaVilla Dairy wagon, circa 1916

point is behind the brick building on the left, though the path is not always well kept.

Continue south on Fischer Place, and veer left as it intersects Lake City Way. Walk to the traffic light at NE 98th Street, cross Lake City, turn right, or north, and proceed to NE 100th Street. Turn left, or west, walk up a slight hill, and descend back to Thornton Creek (past a dead-end sign) and the Knickerbocker Floodplain Improvement project in Kingfisher Natural Area. Walk out on the metal pedestrian bridge that crosses the creek.

❸ The history of this little valley illustrates what happened to many of the city's valleys and their creeks. Loggers cleared out the large trees in the late 1800s, the land was sold, and the owner developed the property, in this case planting an orchard. Decades later, a new owner built three cottages, followed by an additional three homes and two outbuildings, all but one of which was in the floodplain and visible from where you stand. In addition, the landowners channelized the creek into a narrow, riprap-lined waterway, inhospitable to fish and aquatic invertebrates.

Planning to restore the creek, Seattle Public Utilities (SPU) and Seattle Parks purchased all of the property along the creek from the final land-

Restored habitat in Knickerbocker Floodplain, Thornton Creek

owners, the Knickerbockers. The agencies removed all buildings in 2007 and seven years later began to alter the creek so that it flooded less often and offered better habitat for fish. Crews removed invasive vegetation and planted native plants, built a meandering channel, and added large woody debris. They also rebuilt the floodplain by widening and excavating it.

As part of SPU's mandate to reduce flood damage to public facilities and private property and its core mission of improving water quality and habitat in urban streams, the utility agency is at the forefront of floodplain restoration, or what is known as reconnecting the floodplain. During restoration, the creek floodplain is excavated deeply and widely so that it can be filled with a bed of relatively porous rock aggregate. The creek channel then sits in this bed, which acts as a sponge, or what hydrologists call the *hyporheic zone*—the region under and around a stream that aids in sediment filtration, enhances stream flow, and improves nutrient processing. A wider floodplain also gives floodwater space to spread out, slow down, and drop sediment, which translates to fewer downstream problems. This

OPTIONAL SIDE TRIP: A WILD SPACE IN THE CITY

This side trip involves some effort, and you might get dirty.

From the northwest corner of the Knickerbocker Floodplain, continue west on NE 100th Street until it ends at a wooden bridge (wide enough to drive a car across). Cross this bridge over Thornton Creek to a path that leads up the former driveway of one of the houses that was purchased and removed.

This section of the Kingfisher Natural Area was formerly known as Thornton Creek Park 6. To explore the natural area, follow the path, crossing a wet area on logs, boards, and paving stones. The path then winds up and over a fairly steep hillside and ultimately back down to the stream.

The park's name derives from the kingfishers that inhabit the creek and excavate nests in the sandy banks. How far you explore is up to you. Return to the main walk via the same route you've come.

wholesale reconstruction of the Thornton Creek ecosystem was one of the first projects of its kind in the country.

Cross Thornton Creek on the metal bridge, ascend the stairs to NE 98th Street, turn left, and walk east to Lake City Way. (If you don't want to climb the stairway, retrace your steps on 100th Street back to Lake City Way, turn right, or south, and continue to the light.) Cross Lake City, and follow NE 98th Street east and down into a slight dip. (The goal is to get you away from the noise of Lake City Way.)

❹ To the south is the former property of the Nishitani family, who ran Oriental Gardens Nursery on this site from 1912 to 1969. Denjiro Nishitani arrived in Seattle from Japan in 1906, began work as a dishwasher, and then became a groundskeeper before starting his greenhouse. He eventually was able to bring over the rest of his family, who helped him manage the business until 1942 when they were forced into internment camps during World War II. After the war, the Nishitanis returned to the nursery, which had been run for them by sympathetic associates, and operated it until the death of the eldest son.

Oriental Gardens Nursery, operated by the Nishitani family, 1916

Walk east to Ravenna Avenue, turn left, or north, and continue to NE 105th Street. Along the way, look across Ravenna for a pair of tall sequoia trees (which have a more triangular shape than our native conifers) and a row of taller, narrow Lombardy poplars. (Tree expert Arthur Lee Jacobson describes the poplars as "the ubiquitous exclamation point of trees." Settlers typically planted them as a windbreak, often along property lines.) Turn right, or east, at 105th and ascend a slight hill to a kiosk at 32nd Avenue NE.

❺ To the north, the grassy slope drops through a grove of trees to Meadowbrook Playfield. Part of the slope is home to a "guerrilla" orchard and edible hedge, planted without city permission in the 1990s. The plantings include apple, cherry, peach, pear, persimmon, plum, and quince. The trees, as well as vegetable and other fruit gardens, are now established and maintained by the Meadowbrook Community Garden and Orchard, which donates most of the produce to local food banks.

Continue east on 105th Street, and cross 35th Avenue NE. At 36th Avenue, access a paved trail on the left, or north, side of the road. Continue east on the trail as it parallels the road, passes a sign for Meadowbrook Pond, and turns the corner at 39th Avenue NE. (You will circle back through the pond area at the next stop.)

❻ In May 1859, surveyors working for the General Land Office noted an "Indian trail" near a narrow stream (roughly where 105th and Thornton Creek are today). They also recorded a fish trap in the stream, about one block east of where you stand.

Historian David Buerge told me that the Indian trail was used by the Native people, the *Tu-oh-beh-DAHBSH,* or people of the Tu-oh-bed (a Native name for Thornton). They had a small settlement at the mouth of Thornton (in modern-day Matthews Beach) and traveled from Lake Washington west to the bog near the headwaters of the south fork of Thornton. The trail probably influenced the layout of 105th a few blocks to the east, where the road curves and becomes 106th Street before continuing east to the lake. "One can easily imagine the trail being widened into a dirt road, houses being built beside, and city engineers deciding it made more sense to simply pave the curvy street than plow a straight one through peoples' property," says Buerge.

Follow the paved trail north as it crosses over Thornton Creek and continues along Meadowbrook Pond. The trail soon reaches a T-intersection. Turn left, or west, onto a walkway over the pond.

❼ Meadowbrook Pond is a nine-acre site with a detention pond built between 1996 and 1998 for flood control. Historically a wetland, Meadowbrook was the location of the Lake City Wastewater Treatment Plant

THORNTON CREEK'S TRIBUTARIES

Thornton Creek has more named tributaries than any creek in the city. They are Evergreen (named for the plant), Hamlin (for the family), Kramer (unknown), Little Brook (size), Littles (family), Matthews (family), Mock (family), Sacagawea (school), Victory (neighborhood), and Willow (plant). Evergreen is now known as Meridian, and Thornton has also been called Fisher or Fischer.

from 1952 until 1967 when the city concentrated all sewage treatment at West Point. The abandoned property and buildings became storage areas for Nathan Hale High School and also housed the students' auto shop. Extra monorail track from the 1962 World's Fair also ended up on the property. In the late 1980s, local activists began to push city officials to redevelop the site, leading to demolition of the former treatment plant in 1990. Several years of debate and meetings resulted in a plan for restored wetlands, an art garden, a wildlife refuge, and the central feature, a detention pond.

The pond has been a great success with many native birds and mammals returning to their historic habitats, but there was also a problem. Too much sediment entered the pond, which forced SPU to do minor cleaning every 3 to 5 years and a full-scale dredging every 10 years or so. This sediment overload occurred because of channelizing Thornton Creek at the confluence of its north and south forks. To avoid recurrent problems, SPU dredged and expanded the pond in 2012 to 2013 and completely restructured the floodplain of the confluence in 2014. As with the restoration in the Knickerbocker reach, SPU excavated and widened the confluence floodplain to slow the water, provide room for flooding, and improve fish habitat. These efforts are known as the Thornton Creek Confluence Floodplain Reconnection project.

> At the end of the walkway, follow the paved path right to where four paths intersect. Walk straight across to the path that curves out of sight. In about 150 yards, it returns you to the parking lot of the Meadowbrook Community Center. Before crossing over to the parking lot, turn right and walk up 35th Avenue NE to a bridge across Thornton Creek for a fine view of the confluence restoration area. The next numbered stop corresponds to the view over this confluence. (A right turn at the four-way intersection leads to a partial view of this work.)

❽ Far from a healthy waterway, Thornton Creek has high fecal coliform counts, compromised habitat, and a surrounding landscape of impervious surfaces. And yet we, as a city, have chosen to spend tens of millions of dollars on the restoration of Thornton Creek and other creeks in the city. They will never be pristine or even very close to their predevelopment condition. They will never be full of salmon, and the few salmon they do attract will have little effect on the overall health and survival of the fish species as a whole. One can argue that the money spent on creeks could be better spent on other pressing urban needs, such as social services and education, but environmental health is also a pressing urban need.

These projects are prioritized for several reasons. Public agencies must ensure health and safety; flood prevention is a key way to meet this goal, and it saves money in the long run. Agencies also have to follow federal and state regulations, more and more of which require mitigation and restoration. Seattleites also demand these projects. Outreach sessions with residents conducted by SPU have revealed that they consider improving habitat a high priority and one that they are willing to pay for. They believe that a focus on the environment makes Seattle a more livable city and one better prepared for climate change.

Among the reasons residents support restoration is that the creeks provide hope for city dwellers, who see that when given a chance, native plants can survive and flourish in the urban environment. In addition, native fish are returning and making use of the improved habitat, even if they are not flourishing. If animals and plants can do this here, then surely they can return to wilder places. And on a more practical note, restoration has led to a reduction in sediment load and property damage caused by flooding.

In addition, the long-term public focus on these projects helps residents become aware of the creeks, their natural and human histories, and the benefits to be gained through restoration. After people become more aware, they are more likely to approve of similar projects in other parts of the city and in wilder places. Creeks also help people connect with the natural world and the place they live and ultimately can bring a community together, fostering better relationships and a more resilient neighborhood.

Magnuson Park

THE LAND COMES FULL CIRCLE

This walk through one of Seattle's largest parks offers a chance to see a fine example of large-scale landscape restoration.

DISTANCE	3.5 miles
START/END	E 1 parking lot in Warren G. Magnuson Park near the intersection of NE 65th Street and Lake Shore Drive NE
NOTES	Restrooms are located throughout the park. The walk traverses a couple of stretches of hard-packed dirt trail and passes by many spots where you might want to wander off and explore more.

Magnuson Park exemplifies our changing relationship with the land. First surveyed in 1855, the peninsula has been homesteaded, logged, leveled, drained, and paved. But in the past two decades the land has also been replanted, revitalized, and restored, in the process becoming one of the gems of Seattle's park system. Few other ecosystems in Seattle have experienced such change and renewal.

Known by settlers as the Sand Point peninsula, the area originally had rolling topography covered in Douglas fir (six feet in diameter), western red cedar, western hemlock, and red alder. Early federal surveyors also found

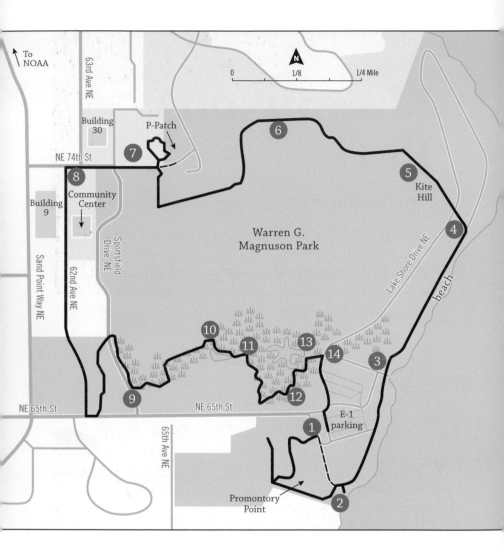

two narrow streams flowing into a shallow bay (named Pontiac by an early landowner from Pontiac, Michigan) at the north end and a swamp to the south. Within the swamp, they observed a body of water, initially unnamed but soon labeled Mud Lake.

Aerial view of naval station, May 1953

By the 1870s, homesteaders had arrived, and in 1886 Edward Lee opened the first business on the point, a boat-building company. Lee primarily provided vessels for the extensive fleet of steamboats and paddle-wheelers that ferried passengers around the lake. Three years later, the Pontiac Brick & Tile Company arrived. To move bricks, it utilized the Seattle Lake Shore and Eastern Railway (now the route of the Burke-Gilman Trail), which stopped at the town of Pontiac on Pontiac Bay. The factory soon employed enough men that the Pontiac post office opened in 1890. But brick making was not a long-term growth industry, and by 1914, the factory had shut down. At the time around 150 people lived in Pontiac and on Sand Point.

The biggest change to the landscape began in 1920 when King County acquired 220 acres of Sand Point for Seattle's first airfield. (The first successful circumnavigation of the world by air started from the airfield on April 6, 1924. Four flyers departed, and two returned on September 28.) By 1926, when it deeded 400 acres to the Navy, the county had acquired most of the rest of the peninsula. After the government decided it no longer needed the space, the city took over the land in the 1970s. It was renamed in honor of Senator Warren G. Magnuson in 1977. The base officially closed in September 1995, with the City Council approving a master plan that included a wetland and sports fields in 2004.

Start at the parks department sign for Promontory Point, which is on a road that is separated from the west side of the E-1 parking lot by a row of trees. The lot is at the east end of NE 65th Street adjacent to the boat ramp. Signs along 65th indicate Promontory Point.

❶ Promontory Point is one of the least visited areas of Magnuson. The Navy used it as a quarry for fill material and as a firing range. (There were designated targets, but many trees suffered at the hands of shooters.) Neglected for years, the point was overrun with invasive plants, but in the late 1990s a multiyear project began the restoration of the site. Volunteers planted native species, removed invasives, and established a trail system. There is also a native plant and butterfly garden, where you might see species such as western tiger swallowtail, mourning cloak, and Lourquin's admirals.

If you wish to explore the point, here's a short tour, which has one steepish, stair-stepped hill to ascend. (If you decide not to explore the point, continue south on the road [dashed line on map] by the pavilion, and follow it as it curves around to a series of black limestone columns [number 2 on map]). Walk west through the pavilion to a narrow path, which connects to a wide gravel path. Turn right and go uphill past snowberries (which have white berries) and vine maples to a level open area (the location of the former naval quarry). The bluff to the right has been used by kingfishers for nesting; the birds excavate one- to eight-foot-long tunnels in the sandy bank. Follow the trail south. It will soon start to ascend and curve up a stepped pathway. At the top is an intersection of several trails and a good spot to see native madronas, with their characteristic smooth red bark and dark green leaves. Take the right-hand path, which extends about 125 yards to a point that offers good views of the park when no leaves are on the trees. (One longtime birder at the park calls this area "warbler alley" for the number and varieties of warblers he regularly sees here. Also look for shelf fungus, which grows on dead trees.)

Return to the intersection, and turn left and descend a relatively steep road/path along a boundary fence. At the bottom, veer left onto a paved road, then turn right and around to a series of black limestone columns.

❷ Perri Lynch Howard's *Straight Shot*, built in 2007, takes advantage of and incorporates the National Geodetic Survey's Sand Point Calibration Baseline. The kilometer-long baseline was set up so that local surveyors could test their electronic equipment on a very precisely measured distance. When the parks department acquired the land, there was concern that

Shelf fungus, Promontory Point

the baseline would be eliminated, but local surveyors prevailed upon the department to protect the corridor via an art project.

In her work, Howard incorporated a dozen columns, each twice the distance from the previous one, except for the final northernmost column, which had to be placed at a different distance so it would not be in the middle of a ball field. The columns run along the calibration baseline. Each column has two holes cut at different levels that let a viewer "mak[e] a targeted observation in the landscape, adopting the stance of a surveyor

Straight Shot, Perri Lynch Howard, 2007

calibrating his instruments," wrote Howard in her concept proposal. Surveyors, police departments, and industry still regularly use the baseline to ensure the accuracy of their devices.

> Return to the road that crosses *Straight Shot* (about 20 feet), turn right, and follow the pavement north along the shoreline. Don't forget to look south at the stellar views of Mount Rainier. Continue past the boat ramp, where there usually are portable toilets, to a small kiosk.

❸ With its diverse habitat, many acres, and accessible shoreline, Magnuson Park is one of the city's finer birding areas. In addition, a seasonal variation in species means that you can return throughout the year and regularly encounter new birds. Along the shoreline, look for buffleheads, mergansers, greater and lesser scaup, mallards, and gadwalls. In winter, the area north around the dock at the swimming beach hosts many different gulls including California, mew, and glaucous. Bald eagles and osprey also hunt over the lake throughout the year.

Lake Washington is the state's second largest natural lake, with about 72 miles of shoreline and an average depth of 110 feet; off the Magnuson shore, the lake drops more than 185 feet. Two rivers—the Cedar and Sammamish—flow into the lake, but no river flows out. The Black River once did, but it disappeared in 1916 with the opening of the ship canal and locks, and the lake's outlet is now the Hiram M. Chittenden Locks (see Walk 9 for more details).

Similar to other lakes in the state, Lake Washington is a product of the last ice age. But its formation was a bit different than those. Nearby Green Lake is a kettle lake, formed by a chunk of ice that melted. Many mountain lakes, known as tarns, developed where glacial ice gouged out a low spot that later filled with water. In contrast, Lake Washington fills a depression excavated by water.

> Continue north to the public swimming beach, where there are also public toilets.

❹ The odd-looking ramp/underground structure to the west is an old magazine, or storage unit for explosives and ammunition, which was situated far from where Navy personnel lived.

To the north is *The Fin Project: From Swords into Plowshares*, an art installation by John T. Young that repurposed diving planes (horizontal

GLACIERS IN SEATTLE

From about 17,400 to 14,500 years ago during the last ice age, a 3,000-foot-thick glacier spread south out of what is now Canada to about Olympia before retreating, or melting, back north. The ice generated several notable features in the landscape. As the ice advanced, streams carried fine-grain sediment into a large lake that covered much of the modern-day Puget lowland. Up to 100 feet thick, the sediment layer is known as the Lawton Clay. It would later become central to Seattle's early brick-making industry. Next to be deposited was the Esperance Sand, a sandy, gravelly layer that can be up to 200 feet thick. And finally atop the pile is the Vashon till, consisting of a mix of sand, gravel, cobbles, and boulders. These three layers make up most of Seattle's hills.

Two other features associated with the ice age are the city's terrestrial topography and its big bodies of water. The first feature developed when the glacier moved south and acted like a giant rake scraping the landscape into the roughly parallel hills and valleys that give Seattleites their great views and challenge their driving skills. These structures primarily run north–south, or the direction traveled by the ice. Lake Washington, Lake Sammamish, and Puget Sound, in contrast, were formed by water flowing under the glacier. Known as subglacial melt, these rivers cut down into the underlying sediments and carved out deep basins, which subsequently filled with water.

fins that aid in submerging and surfacing) from decommissioned US Navy nuclear submarines. Young has said that the inspiration for the project was instantaneous. "I took one look at the fins and said there's no way we are going to cut those up. We are going to use them exactly as they are. They are magnificent forms. And that's when I saw the orca whale dorsal fin." He completed a similar project in Florida.

Ascend the grass slope west of *The Fin Project*. At the top you will be on Kite Hill.

❺ Workers began to create Kite Hill in the early 1970s out of the naval station's old asphalt runways. They finished the hill in 1989 with 40,000 cubic yards of fill excavated from a garage at the Pike Place Market. Over the years, artists have used the hill as a site for guerrilla art, such as nine life-size plywood soldiers and a nine-foot-tall steel monolith. Enjoy the splendid views from on high.

Based on the number of place names, Sand Point peninsula must have been an important location to the area's Native people. One name, *Cha7áhLqoo*, means "digging in the water" and probably refers to wapato (a potato-like tuber) collected in the wetlands around the former Mud Lake. Another, *TudáxWdee*, is the Whulshootseed word for snowberry, a plant used for medicine. And perhaps most significant, *slágWlagWatS* references the inner bark of the cedar tree. Cedars here must have been special as the trees were ubiquitous throughout the region. The final name describes the point, which was called *sqWsub*, or fog.

Continue north on the hill a short way until you intercept a wide path, and turn left, or west. When you soon come to an intersection of trails, go straight to the large field, turn right, and follow the trail around the field until you reach the black column of Perri Lynch Howard's *Straight Shot*.

⑥ To the north is the National Oceanic and Atmospheric Administration's Western Regional Center. The first building opened in 1981. Programs include the National Weather Service, Alaska Fisheries Science Center, and

NATIVE NAMES ON THE LANDSCAPE

Coll Thrush writes in *Native Seattle: Histories from the Crossing-Over Place* that the "four European compass points were not necessarily the most important directions in Puget Sound indigenous life." Instead, Native people placed more importance on features such as weather, food, travel, and local wildlife. In his book, Thrush includes four maps of Seattle, which list over 125 names and their origins. Reading them, one realizes that the original inhabitants had a much different relationship to the landscape than modern dwellers. Unfortunately, only a handful of Native place names have persisted on modern maps. Licton Springs, in north Seattle, is a corruption of *lééQtud* meaning "red paint," in reference to springs colored by rust. Another one is Shilshole, from *sHulsHóól*, or "tucked away inside." All spellings of Native place names throughout the book are from the first edition of Thrush's *Native Seattle*, which contains a pronunciation guide and a history of the origin of the place names. His book uses *Whulshootseed* over the more common *Lushootseed*.

the Pacific Marine Environmental Laboratory, whose research focuses on helping to make more resilient coastlines.

Within the NOAA facility is an art walk consisting of five sculptures. Probably the most famous is Doug Hollis's *A Sound Garden,* which can be seen from Kite Hill. Access to the art walk is through the main gate on NE NOAA Drive off Sand Point Way. Please check the NOAA website for entry requirements. www.wrc.noaa.gov.

> Continue counterclockwise around the field until you come to an intersection, turn right, and walk on a wide path, which soon runs along a turf field. Walk along the field to a gravel path on the right. Take it to the parking lot, turn right, walk to a road, and cross it at the crosswalk. Take the narrow path to the right, which soon crosses a small bridge, and continue into the Magnuson Park P-Patch.

❼ Begun in 1973 as an outgrowth of a farm run by the Picardo family at 25th Avenue NE and NE 80th Street, Seattle's P-Patch program includes more than 85 community gardens. Take the time to explore these gardens, but do not pick any food.

> Exit the P-Patch under a large wooden trellis. Descend the stairs to a small amphitheater (west of the garden), and follow the path around the circle to the west side. Before you is the former brig, or the Navy base's jail. Take the first left (at a piece of art titled *Geometric Garden in Red*), and walk by the children's garden to the crosswalk you recently crossed. Turn right, or west, at the road. *Watch for traffic—there is no sidewalk for the first 100 yards or so.* Look for a sidewalk, and follow it west across a roadway. To the north is Building 30, formerly an aircraft hangar. Continue west, and cross 63rd Avenue NE to 62nd Avenue NE.

❽ The next half mile goes past a variety of former Navy buildings. They are part of the City of Seattle–designated Sand Point Historic District, which was approved in 2011. The district includes the very large Building 9 (barracks for enlisted men), which as of 2016 was slated for development into low-income housing, on the west side and Building 47 (recreation building, now Magnuson Community Center) on the east side. Most buildings south of the community center are owned by Solid Ground, a nonprofit working "to end poverty and undo racism and other oppressions that are root causes of poverty." Its buildings provide transitional and permanent housing along with case management for families and individuals. As of 2016, Solid Ground had more than 150 units within the park.

In addition, four barn owl nest boxes are located in the district. They were built because renovation forced the owls out of several older buildings. As of 2016, the boxes had been nested in regularly by the owls, key predators of the park's rodents.

Walk south on 62nd to a T-intersection at NE 65th Street, turn left, and walk about 100 feet to a dirt path that leads north into the trees. Follow the path, which will take you about 250 yards north to a paved road. Cross at the crosswalk to the Mickey Merriam Athletic Complex, turn right, or south, and follow a paved trail along the wetlands. In about 150 yards, veer left onto a gravel trail, and follow it until it intersects a paved path.

❾ The wetlands you have been walking by and will continue to pass were constructed in 2008 and 2009 as part of an integrated plan to develop wetlands, athletic fields, and transition zones. In addition to providing new habitat, the restoration project helps filter and clean storm water and acts as a sponge so that rainwater slowly percolates into the wetlands.

The wetlands consist of four parts. Storm water enters through the entrance marsh system you just walked by. Beyond the ball field that you will soon pass are the marsh ponds (aka the rice paddies), shallow water areas that fill seasonally. They provide habitat for Pacific chorus frogs, migratory shorebirds, and numerous insects. The larger, permanently wet promontory ponds are up to 10 feet deep. They are a good spot to find waterfowl, amphibians, beaver, and insects such as dragonflies and damselflies (24 species as of 2015, the most at any single locality in Seattle, though the number is now decreasing because increased vegetation leads to less available water). In 2011, work began on the final section, shore ponds, which created a closer link between Lake Washington and the older wetlands.

Walk north on the paved path toward a baseball field. Just before the field, veer right on a paved path, and walk along the south side of the Frank Papasedero Field. At the end of the field, there is a gravel path. (A short detour to the left up a narrow side trail leads to the top of a low berm and good views over the wetlands complex.) Follow the gravel path to the right to a T-intersection near a bench.

Eight-spotted skimmer, Libellula forensis

⑩ The next section takes you between the final entrance marsh and the marsh ponds. Depending upon the time of year and the amount of precipitation, these shallow ponds may be dry. On your right are cattails and sedges, two plants found in wetlands. You will also pass by many red alders, which in spring often host many aphids. They, in turn, are prey for adult ladybird beetles, or ladybugs, and their alligator-shaped larvae.

Follow the trail south, or right, from the bench. Turn left when the trail forks again (the right-hand fork leads toward a parking lot), and continue until you reach a bench and a large decaying stump.

⑪ You have now reached the deep, permanent promontory ponds. The nest boxes across the water are for little brown and big brown bats, the park's most common bat species. Five boxes have been placed in the park. Birds to see around the ponds include yellow-rumped warbler, American goldfinch, Virginia rail, sora, red-spotted towhee, marsh wren, red-winged blackbird, merlin, song sparrow, common yellowthroat, black phoebe, pied-billed grebe, and junco.

Also look for beaver signs, such as gnawed-off branches and trunks and drag marks across the trail where the beavers pull debris from one pond to the next. As of 2015, there were at least six beavers in the ponds. They had built a 7-foot-high lodge and an 80-foot-long dam.

In the snags, all of which were placed during the restoration process, look for the holes of flickers and furrows hewn by pileated woodpeckers.

> Turn right, walk to another T-intersection, and turn left. Continue around the pond, past an intersection that leads to a road, to a junction with a trail that leads east to a grove of trees.

⓬ The grove consists of black cottonwoods. These trees were not planted as part of the restoration process but seeded themselves in the years since the Navy stopped using the airfield.

> Turn left at the intersection. In about 50 feet is one of the best views into the largest open water in the promontory pond area, as well as a sign describing the ponds. Continue past the sign to a junction where the trail wraps around a small island (about 10 feet wide) of shrubs.

⓭ Note how the trail is raised slightly. This area flooded in the wet winter of 2014–15 after which the parks department decided that the trail should be higher.

> Turn right and follow the trail to a road. Cross it. On your right is a stair-step sculpture, which leads to the top of a berm and great views into the wetlands. The steps line up with the naval station's 5,050-foot-long main runway (now removed).

⓮ Magnuson Park is an unusual park. It is one of three park spaces in Seattle—the others are Discovery and South Lake Union—previously owned by the United States military. Modern visitors benefit enormously from this early federal ownership, as it is not too hard to imagine that if the government had not acquired these properties, each would probably have ended up in private hands and thus been inaccessible to the public. These spaces are among the curious artifacts of the military's former presence in Seattle, remnants that the city and residents are taking advantage of as they develop creative public spaces.

Follow the road south back to where you parked in lot E-1. *Be careful: many cars travel this road on weekends.*

Capitol Hill

ELEGANCE IN THE DETAILS

This exploration of the north end of Capitol Hill passes by stately homes, a grand park, and a lesser-known cemetery.

DISTANCE   2.8 miles
START/END 15th Avenue E and E Garfield Street
NOTES   Volunteer Park has several public restrooms. The walk includes one very short side trip.

Between 1890 and 1900, Seattle evolved from a town to a city. In this decade, it experienced its first great boom with the Klondike Gold Rush, started to develop trade routes to Asia, and became the leading general manufacturing center in the Pacific Northwest. In addition, the population nearly doubled to about 81,000 residents. With the new economy came new money and people of means who needed homes to live in.

Housing had boomed across the city in response to the growth, but one large piece of land remained undeveloped: 160 acres of a "large and sightly natural park" that was on the northeast section of what was then called Broadway Hill. According to the *Seattle Times,* it was the "only piece of platable land of any magnitude remaining" in the city. Until 1890, the property had been owned by the estate of Selim Woodworth, a veteran of the Mexican-American War, who never saw his property. The acreage came into Woodworth's possession through a bounty land warrant, which granted soldiers the right to obtain free land in the public domain. On July 10, 1900, James A. Moore paid $225,000 for the Woodworth tract, which stretched from Roy to Galer Streets and from 15th to 23rd Avenues.

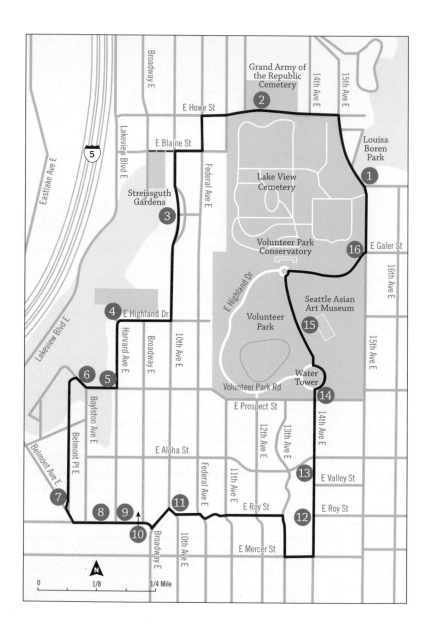

Moore began selling his "strictly first class" property for "men of means" on October 25, 1901. In the year since he had bought Woodworth's land, Moore had graded and paved the streets with concrete and asphalt, laid water mains and sewers, and poured concrete sidewalks. He had also named the area Capitol Hill. Why he did so is one of Seattle's niggling conundrums. The name could have originated with a neighborhood bearing the same name in Denver, where Moore's wife had lived, or perhaps Moore had hoped to site the state capitol building on his hill. Historian Jacqueline B. Williams, however, notes in *The Hill with a Future: Seattle's Capitol Hill 1900–1946* that there was little chance of the latter happening. She thinks Moore's name was merely a shrewd idea on his part to promote his development. If so, the plan worked: he sold at least 125 lots to 64 people in the first month of sales. Most lots cost $1,000.

Start at Louisa Boren Park.

❶ With its great views out to Lake Washington, Union Bay, and the Cascade Mountains, Louisa Boren Park is a hidden little treasure on Capitol Hill. It is also home to several historic trees, English oaks that grow along the drop-off on the eastern edge of the park, across the path from Lee Kelly's large, unnamed sculpture. Seattle Parks Department historian Don Sherwood wrote that the trees were originally planted at Denny Park and were moved here in 1930 when Denny Park was lowered during the final regrade of Denny Hill. No other trees that grew at Denny before the regrade are known to exist.

This small park honors one of Seattle's earliest citizens. Born in Illinois in 1827, Louisa Boren arrived here on November 13, 1851, as part of the Denny Party, the group of settlers who are considered the founders of Seattle. She was single at the time but soon married David Denny in the first settler wedding in the city. Because she had carried sweetbriar rose seeds from her home, she was known as the Sweetbriar Bride. Louisa's other claim to fame is that she was the last survivor of the Denny Party (she died in August 1916).

Walk north one block on 15th Avenue E, and turn left, or west, on E Howe Street. Continue west until you come to the Grand Army of the Republic Cemetery on the north side of the road.

❷ The Grand Army of the Republic (GAR) was a fraternal organization set up to aid Union veterans of the Civil War. In 1896, five local GAR posts united to acquire land from Huldah and David Kaufman and establish a cemetery for the veterans and their wives. There are 526 graves—mostly of Union soldiers including three black soldiers (which was unusual for its era); GAR accepted any soldier's remains as long as they were of a Civil War veteran. A couple of Confederate veterans are also buried here. The vast majority of the interred soldiers died in or near Seattle. The Seattle Parks Department now manages the cemetery with the help of a neighborhood group. To get a feel for the layout of the tombstones, walk to the obelisk, which was placed by the Woman's Relief Corps.

Walk west on E Howe Street to Federal Avenue E, and turn left, or south. Walk one block to E Blaine Street, and turn right, or west. Walk to 10th Avenue E, and cross to the west side of the street. For a short but energetic side trip to a little urban oasis, walk west on Blaine and descend 70 steps to the Streiss-guth Gardens (after 35 steps, you will see a dirt path leading into the garden, but the main part of the park lies lower). Started by the Streissguth family, this garden is now owned by the city. To continue on the main route, walk south on 10th to the Office of the Bishop of the Episcopal Church of Western Washington.

❸ This grand building was originally the home of John and Eliza Leary. Leary arrived in Seattle in 1869 and soon became involved in numerous development projects including coal mines in Renton, a water supply company in Seattle, and ownership of the *Seattle Post* (which eventually became the *Seattle Post-Intelligencer*). He was also Seattle's mayor from 1884 to 1885 as a member of the Business Men's Ticket party. He married Eliza Ferry, daughter of Washington state's first governor, Elisha Ferry, in 1891.

In 1903, Leary hired Alfred Bodley to design a house for him and his wife. Unfortunately, he died before the house was finished. Eliza, who was well known for hosting many events at the house, lived there until her death in 1935. The lovely sandstone used in the construction of the house came from Tenino, Washington, one of three areas that supplied most of the local stone used in building projects across the region. It is a 50-million-year-old sandstone, deposited when what we now think of as the I-5 corridor was oceanfront property and the Olympic Mountains did not exist.

During World War II, the American Red Cross acquired the Leary house and used it as its headquarters with training rooms, dormitories for evacuees, and a home-nursing department. After the war, the house passed to the Episcopal Diocese of Olympia. Curiously, the bishop decided to remove a couple of the house's most famous features, two glass windows (16 by 8 feet and 8 by 8 feet) designed by Louis Comfort Tiffany. The bishop donated them to the Burke Museum, noting that they made the house's great hall look too much like a funeral parlor. The Burke still owns them and plans to have them on display in their new museum.

Next door to the south is the former home of Eliza's brother, Pierre, which includes several carved wooden owls. Historically, this area was known as "owl hollow" because owls nested in the surrounding trees. When you pass the gates, look for the two modern sculptures of owls.

One additional detail of note: 10th Avenue curves slightly around the former Leary property. Historically, 10th did not go north past this point and instead ended at a cul de sac that led into Leary's driveway.

Peacock with hollyhocks and morning glories, Tiffany Studios, 1903

The modern road is not straight because Leary and other nearby land owners didn't want the road to cross their land. An article in the *Seattle Daily Bulletin* reported that Leary's group eventually sided with city engineers but on the condition that "unsightly poles, billboards, and other nuisances and street cars are to be kept off" the new road.

Continue south on 10th, turn right on E Highland Drive, and walk on the north side of the street to just past Broadway E. On your right is the former Sam Hill mansion.

❹ Samuel Hill was a lawyer and railroad executive who worked primarily for and with his father-in-law, James J. Hill. The younger Hill moved to Seattle in 1901 and soon became involved in a variety of investments. He is probably best known for building his Maryhill Mansion and Stonehenge Memorial (in southern Washington on the Columbia River, 10 miles south of Goldendale). Hill began work on his Capitol Hill home in 1908. According to a *Seattle Times* article, he built it in part to host Crown Prince Albert Leopold of Belgium, whom Hill had invited to Seattle for the Alaska-Yukon-Pacific Exposition. Unfortunately for Hill, politics kept Leopold from visiting Seattle.

Made of concrete, the walls are 10 feet thick at the base and reinforced with massive steel rails. On top of the house was a rooftop garden where guests could eat dinner in a park-like setting. Other novel features included a telephone in each room, a gas-powered heating plant, and a single switch in the master bedroom that could turn on all the lights in the house. Note the small sundial on the southeastern corner of the house (above a gate). The quote on the dial is from Rowland Hazard, a woolen manufacturer and friend of Hill's from Rhode Island, who had a sundial on his house.

Follow Highland Drive as it curves left, and walk south on Harvard Avenue E to E Prospect Street.

❺ Horace Chapin Henry, a wealthy railroad builder, originally owned the 1.6-acre hedge-lined property that encompasses the northwest corner of the intersection. The estate included a large mansion, stables, and private art gallery, all of which were demolished and eventually replaced in the 1950s with a more modern house. The Henry Gallery on the University of Washington campus started with Henry's donation of his art collection. After his death, Henry's sons donated the house and property to the city for a library on Capitol Hill in honor of their mother, Susan J. Henry. The library board had neither the money to renovate the mansion for a library nor to pay the 90 dollars a month necessary for upkeep of the grounds. In 1953, the board sold the property to pay for the site of the present Capitol Hill Branch of the library, which was initially known as the Susan J. Henry Branch.

Turn right, or west, on E Prospect Street, and walk one block to Boylston Avenue E.

❻ You are now in the heart of the federally and city designated Harvard-Belmont Historic District, an area bounded roughly by E Highland Drive, Belmont Avenue E, E Roy Street, and Broadway E. Starting in the 1890s, the area became a premier location for wealthy Seattleites to build large homes, often in an English country-manor style. Architectural historian Larry Kreisman says the Old World–style was popular for "substantial, sophisticated homes of the well-to-do, [which gave] the nouveau riche the appearance of long-held ties to the land and the city." Many of these estates covered four, six, or more lots. Although nearly all of the original families have moved away, more than 50 homes in the district have architectural and/or historical significance.

To get a good feel for the houses in the district, turn right and follow Prospect around to Belmont Place E. Most of the houses are historic. Walk south on Belmont Place to its intersection with Belmont Avenue E.

❷ To your right, on the corner where the Belmonts intersect, is a large and unusual tree. It is a Garry oak (also known as Oregon white oak), Washington's lone native oak. In 1840 the great botanist David Douglas named the species *Quercus garryana* after Nicholas Garry, a deputy governor for the Hudson's Bay Company. As noted in a sidebar in the Rainier Beach walk (Walk 15), Garry oaks are rare this far north and why this one exists here is unknown, though it was about half its present height in 1928 when the adjacent Oak Manor apartments were built.

Turn left on Belmont Avenue, walk to the intersection, and follow E Roy Street east as it ascends to Boylston Avenue E.

CURBOLOGY

If you take the time to look down at curbs in Seattle, you will be rewarded with a nerdy but novel little story. In early Seattle, 33-million-year-old granite, which came from Index, Washington, was a popular material for curbs because of its hardness and the ease with which it could be cut into square pieces. In the early 1900s a new style of curb began to appear and replace granite curbs. The new curbs were built of concrete with a steel protective rail known as "curb armor," and they were cheaper than stone. Like the granite curbs, the steel rail curbs were eventually replaced—when rubber tires replaced the steel rims of carriage wheels—and are now much less common in Seattle, though they still occur on many corners. Today granite curbs are rare, though the original curbs can also be spotted on corners.

❽ In 1914 Nellie Cornish started the Cornish College of Arts, where she taught piano to children in a single room. When she outgrew that space (at the corner of Broadway and Pine Street), she moved her school to this location in 1921, where she had the present building designed to her specifications. The new school building's appearance was described in the *Town Crier* as having "both the restraint and freedom of Venetian, the Spanish, the Levant, and even of Tibet." At the top of the building are names of famous artists: Anna Pavlova, Russian ballerina; John Millington Synge, Irish playwright and poet; Wilhelm Richard Wagner, German composer; William Morris, British designer; James Abbott McNeill Whistler, American painter. Miss Aunt Nellie, as she was known to people at the school, hoped such luminaries would inspire her students. The bas-relief panels near the building's cornice were modeled on students at the school. Today this building, known as Kerry Hall, houses the Cornish College dance and music department, and the school's main campus is near Westlake Avenue and Denny Way.

Continue east on Roy Street. On the east side of Harvard Avenue E is the Daughters of the American Revolution house.

❾ Seattle's DAR chapter was founded in 1895 and met in members' homes until its membership grew too large. Eliza Ferry Leary guided the development and building of the new bigger space, which was built in 1925 and is a copy of George Washington's home, Mount Vernon. Across the street on the southwest corner of Roy and Harvard Avenue is a small public space consisting of benches and terra-cotta elements. On one of the benches is a large tile bearing an architectural drawing by John Graham, a well-known local architect. The tile also includes a quote from Italo Calvino.

On the southeast corner is the former home of the Woman's Century Club, founded in 1891. Started by 10 women, who "felt its need in the sordid atmosphere of a rapidly developing western city," the club's purpose was "for intellectual culture, original research and the solution of the altruistic problems of the day." By 1925, membership had reached 350 women and the club organized to build the present building. The club still meets regularly though not in this building, which housed the Harvard Exit movie theater for many decades.

Walk east on Roy Street until the end of the block.

⑩ The handsome two-story building on your left is named for its architect Arthur Loveless, who built it in 1931. Described as a "little bit of England" in Seattle, the building centers on a private courtyard surrounded by housing and studio and sales spaces that Loveless hoped would be utilized by local artists. Note the cinder blocks, which were used because they were less expensive than cut stone.

> Continue east, cross to the far side of Broadway, turn left, or north, and follow the road as it curves slightly east. At the corner, turn right, walk east on Roy Street between two brick apartment buildings, and halt at the end of the block.

⑪ Frederick Anhalt is responsible for the apartments on either side of Roy. In the late 1920s, he developed, designed, and built bungalows, commercial buildings, and apartments across Seattle. Anhalt is probably best known for his elegant Capitol Hill apartments with their French Norman inspired elements, such as turrets, arches, and exposed exterior beams, and house like feel created by the addition of a fireplace, usually front and back doors, and often a courtyard garden

> Walk east as Roy Street turns to a path that serpentines between Lowell School and its playfields and continues as Roy Street again. Stay on Roy to 13th Avenue E, and turn right, or south. You will soon pass by the Maryland Apartments, a city-designated landmark built in 1910. Continue south to E Mercer Street, and turn left, or east. Turn left, or north, on 14th Avenue E, and walk one block to E Roy Street.

⑫ You are about to enter what has long been known as "Millionaire's Row," where you will find some of Seattle's finest early-20th-century homes. Built of wood, granite, sandstone, and brick, they display a wide range of styles, though all carry an air of distinction. On the west side of the intersection is a rare sign of early Seattle—a granite hitching post complete with steel ring. During the late 1800s and into the early 1900s, when horses were the main means of travel around the city, hitching posts, such as this one and one just up the block, would have been common and needed.

According to historian Fred Brown, people put up posts because the city had laws against animals running at large, and if an animal strayed, city-hired herders would round up loose livestock, mostly horses and cows, and take them to the cattle pound. In addition, to address concerns about startled horses injuring pedestrians or themselves, the Humane Society

314 – Fourteenth Street, Capitol Hill, Seattle, Washington.

Postcard of the view north on 14th Avenue E, circa 1910

pushed for laws that required teamsters to carry weights that they could attach to horses to keep them from running wild. The other option was to tie the horses to hitching posts.

One block north on the east side of 14th is another remnant of the city's early equestrian history. On the southeast corner of E Valley Street close to the road is a low granite block, or stepping stone. People getting out of horse-drawn carriages would have stepped onto the block and then down to the ground. This block was owned by Elbridge Amos Stuart, who started the Carnation Evaporated Milk Company. He also owned the house behind the stepping stone.

Continue north on 14th Avenue E one block to E Aloha Street.

⓭ The brick mansion (built in 1903) on the southwest corner was the home of Capitol Hill's developer James A. Moore. He also built the Moore Theater in downtown and had a role in regrading the south side of Denny Hill, where he owned the legendary Washington Hotel.

Walk north on 14th Avenue E to Volunteer Park.

⓮ Like many who achieve success late in life, Volunteer Park began rather humbly as 40 acres purchased by the city for a cemetery in 1876. It was

JOHN CHARLES OLMSTED

John Charles Olmsted of Boston's Olmsted Brothers landscape architecture firm arrived in Seattle on April 30, 1903, to design a grand park system. He was arguably the most experienced landscape architect in the country, having begun his career in 1875 when he apprenticed with his stepfather Frederick Law Olmsted, Sr., codesigner of New York's Central Park. Throughout May, the younger Olmsted and his assistant, Percy Jones, traveled across Seattle, surveyed the land, and met with civic leaders. The City Council approved Olmsted's plans in October.

The Olmsted proposal featured a 20-mile-long parkway that ran from Bailey Peninsula (Seward Park) to Fort Lawton (Discovery Park). From Bailey, it snaked along the lake, turned inland to Washington Park and cut across Montlake to the University of Washington. The roadway continued to Ravenna Park and out to Green Lake, up through Woodland Park, and then up, over, and down Queen Anne Hill, with its final extension along the Magnolia bluffs to Fort Lawton. Additional spurs went from Washington Park through Interlaken Park to Volunteer; up Mount Baker Boulevard from Lake Washington; and on Cheasty Boulevard, on the east side of Beacon Hill. Although Olmsted's complete parkway was never implemented, Seattle's citizens passed bonds for park construction and acquisition totaling 3.5 million dollars (the equivalent of about $224 million in 2015) in the eight years following the original proposal.

named Washelli, a Makah word meaning "west wind." In 1887, the City Council decided that the land would better serve as space for the living. It had all the graves removed and the former cemetery was renamed Lake View Park. That name didn't last either; it became City Park and finally Volunteer, in 1901, the same year the reservoir was built.

Eight years later, park designer John Charles Olmsted wrote that as Volunteer "will be surrounded by a highly finished style of city development, it will be best to adopt a neat and smooth style of gardening throughout." The implementation of Olmsted's plans finally led to the park becoming one of the city's most popular public spaces.

In front of you is the brick water tower (built in 1906), or stand pipe, whose internal tank holds 883,000 gallons. Inside the tower, winding around the tank, are 106 steps up to an observation area with views of the city—best in winter when leaves don't block the scenery—and an excellent display about the city's park system (open to the public). As with the other stand pipes around Seattle (for example, on Queen Anne Hill and in West Seattle and Magnolia), it was built on a high point, a necessity because gravity is the main force feeding water from the city's reservoirs into surrounding homes.

> Follow the main road, which splits around the water tower, as it leads north into the park.

⓯ On the right is the original Seattle Art Museum, which opened in 1933 with money provided by Margaret MacTavish Fuller and her son Richard, who directed the museum for 40 years. It now houses the Seattle Asian Art Museum. Architectural historians consider it a very progressive design for its time because it broke away from the traditional neoclassical style that then prevailed in the design of most American museums. The building's sandstone came from the Wilkeson quarry near Mount Rainier. It is another of the three principal suppliers of sandstone in western Washington. Chuckanut, near Bellingham, is the third.

North of the museum is the Volunteer Park Conservatory, which opened in 1912. The city purchased it as a kit from Hitchings & Company in New York and assembled the metal frame with its 3,426 glass panes on site. The design is based on London's Crystal Palace. Housed in the conservatory is an enticing collection of cacti, orchids, bromeliads, and palms that is ever-changing and always delightful. In recent years, restoration has focused on returning the building to its historic appearance.

> From the conservatory, turn right, or east, to go out of the park and down to 15th Avenue E. Turn left, or north, on 15th and look across the street at the bus stop on the west side.

⓰ Note the concrete blocks of the retaining wall. Each block has one or two holes. In the former streetcar system that ran down 15th, the trolley's steel rails sat atop and were attached to the slabs. The Capitol Hill line opened in November 1901. As was true of other early Seattle trolley routes, a big impetus for this route's construction was to promote the sale of adjacent real estate. Within a few years, other lines opened on the hill. Not coincidentally, most of the modern bus routes that traverse Capitol Hill, including those that run along Summit, Broadway, 15th, 19th, and 24th, follow

Capitol Hill street trolley, 15th Avenue E and E Aloha Street, 1903

the historic trolley routes. By 1941, all of the streetcars on Capitol Hill and throughout the city had been replaced by buses.

Lake View Cemetery across the street to the west is one of the oldest in the city and one of the most diverse with its graves of city settlers such as Arthur Denny, Henry Yesler, and Doc Maynard; Chief Seattle's daughter Kikisebloo (aka Princess Angeline); Bruce Lee and his son Brandon; a horse named Buck; and Madam Damnable, who ran an early brothel and earned her name for her proclivity for profanity.

Continue one block north to Louisa Boren Park, where you began this walk.

With its elegant houses, well-manicured park, and stately cemeteries, the north end of Capitol Hill continues to exude an air of distinction that would please James Moore. However, like most parts of the city, the hill has changed, becoming more diverse economically and culturally, which has certainly helped it to retain its popularity. But certain fundamental aspects have not changed since Moore's time. People still desire well-built homes, proximity to downtown, and access to public transportation. As they say, the more things change, the more they stay the same.

Beacon Hill

GREAT DIVERSITY AND GREAT VIEWS

Walk by little known overlooks, handsome historic architecture, and curious remnants of city engineering.

DISTANCE	3.2 miles
START/END	Dr. Jose Rizal Park (1007 12th Avenue S)
NOTES	Restrooms are available at numerous businesses and the public library.

Ethnically diverse and geographically isolated (though by artificial means), Beacon Hill has a long history often overlooked by those who do not know the neighborhood. For instance, the earliest white settlers in King County, Luther M. Collins, Henry Van Asselt, and brothers Jacob and Samuel Maple (also spelled Mapel), who arrived in the area two months before the much better-known members of the Denny Party, filed some of the first federal land claims on acreage that is now part of Beacon Hill. Other early claimants were John C. Holgate and Edward Hanford.

Beacon Hill can further claim the first roads in the area. Road No. 1 of King County went over the hill from Seattle to Fort Steilacoom (a few miles south of modern-day Tacoma). Better known was the Military Road, which also connected Seattle to the fort. A third route, the Beach Road, ran along the western edge of Beacon Hill, and is now the route of Airport Way. Due to challenging winter conditions, the Beach Road was used primarily in summer for access to and from Seattle.

The hill was also one of the first places in the county where African Americans owned land. In 1869, a group of African American investors

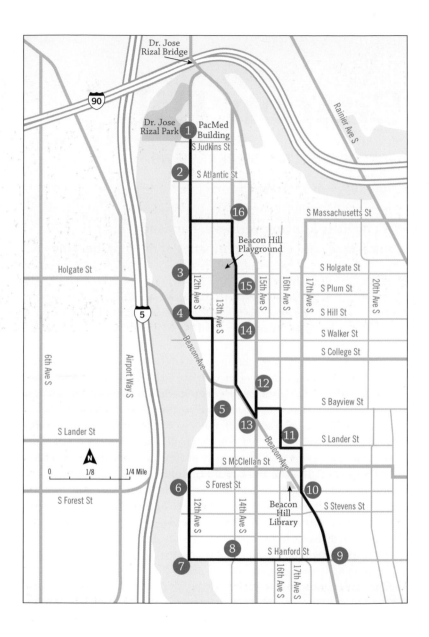

Seattle skyline from Dr. Jose Rizal Bridge

from Portland, Oregon, purchased part of Edward Hanford's land claim. Although most of the investors did not move to Seattle, their purchase started a long wave of minorities, including Japanese, Chinese, Filipinos, and Italians, who have moved to the hill, making it one of Seattle's most diverse neighborhoods.

Beacon Hill's geographic isolation came about during the Dearborn Street Regrade (1909–12). Prior to that project, Beacon connected north to the city via a ridge. During the regrade, water cannons removed more than a million cubic yards of sediment to create the 100-foot-deep canyon now crossed by the Dr. Jose Rizal Bridge, originally known as the 12th Street Bridge.

Start at Dr. Jose Rizal Park on 12th Avenue S on Beacon Hill.

❶ One of the great viewpoints of Seattle, this small green space became park property in 1971. Three years later members of the local Filipino community, part of which centered on Beacon Hill, worked with city govern-

View of northeast corner of tideflats from roughly the location of present-day Dr. Jose Rizal Park, 1881

ment to name the park in honor of Dr. Jose Rizal, a Filipino social reformer, ophthalmologist, poet, and novelist who was executed in 1896 by the Spanish colonial authorities in Manila when he was 35 years old. If you want the best views, come in winter when the park's forest of red alders and bigleaf maples have dropped their leaves.

Across the street is the former US Marine Hospital, which opened in 1933 to serve veterans, merchant seamen, and the Coast Guard. Note the Art Deco setbacks and creative use of brick and terra-cotta, which are supposed to evoke a mountain-like appearance. The hospital eventually became part of the US Public Health Services hospital system after which employees started to work more with underserved populations including Native Americans and Alaskan Natives. Researchers at the hospital also did pioneering studies and patient care in diabetes, bone-marrow transplants, and HIV/AIDS. In 1983, the building became the Pacific Medical Center, or PacMed, the name it was known by when a local developer leased the building and sublet it to Amazon.com. The building now houses a satellite campus of Seattle Central College.

Walk south on 12th Avenue on the west side of the road past S Judkins Street. About halfway down the block is a sequoia tree with an impressive girth. Note the two buildings made of river cobbles behind the tree. Continue to the end of the block and Katie Black's Garden.

❷ Frank D. Black became Seattle's mayor on March 16, 1896. He resigned on April 6, stating he was "fearful that my health, which is never robust, would not endure the worries incident to the administration of public office." Apparently he wasn't that ill, as he lived another 24 years, which gave him time to build an estate at this location. Legend holds that he offered his wife, Katie, a grand tour of Europe in 1913, but she requested instead that he build an elaborate Japanese garden with cobble-clad walls and stairs, tea house, gatehouse, and beehive-shaped milk cooler. The historic garden, pillars, milk cooler, and gatehouse are all that remain of the former three-acre property.

Continue south on 12th Avenue to S Holgate Street.

❸ Look east up Holgate to see an unusual sight in Seattle. Between the 1890s and 1910s, road builders in Seattle regularly paved streets with sandstone cobbles. The small town of Wilkeson, 45 miles southeast of Seattle, provided most of the stone, which made good traction for horses. Although horse shoes did wear down the stone, the cobbles lasted longer and created less of a mess than the mud or wood roads of the past. By 1993, fewer than a hundred cobblestone streets remained in Seattle; the rest had been paved over.

Holgate Street honors John C. Holgate, who arrived in the Duwamish River valley in 1852. He soon wrote his sister to encourage her to move to Seattle, which she did, along with her husband, Edward Hanford. Both Holgate and the Hanfords filed land claims on territory that would initially be called Holgate and Hanford Hill but is better known today as Beacon Hill. It was also known as Reservoir Hill, for a reservoir that used to exist between Plum and Holgate Streets and 13th and 14th Avenues.

Continue south on 12th Avenue past S Plum Street to a tiny green space with a superb panoramic view of the Duwamish River valley.

❹ An often overlooked part of Seattle, the areas known as SODO (South of the Dome/Downtown) and Georgetown have long been the center of industry for the city. From here look west to see the cranes of Harbor Island, the towers and domes of a cement factory, the West Seattle bridge, and acres of warehouses and buildings that house a wide array of manufacturing.

Follow 12th Avenue south as it curves onto S Hill Street. Go right, or south, on 13th Avenue S, and walk south on 13th until it dead-ends at Beacon Avenue S. Carefully cross Beacon, and continue south on 13th as it descends to a more level section.

❺ Note the retaining wall on the east, or left, side of the street. Like many other such walls in Seattle, it's an early example of recycling. The wall is made from material (the best examples are toward the south end of the wall) formerly used in the city's old streetcar trolley system, which was shut down and replaced by buses in 1941. Workers then tore out the system's 230 miles of old rails and concrete slabs (the rails were attached to the slabs) and incorporated them into retaining walls and stairways. At the far end of the wall is an unusual section that features the full length of a single trolley rail. The trees growing out of the wall and wrapping around the rail are Lombardy poplars, a fast-growing tree native to Europe.

Walk south on 13th Avenue to S McClellan Street, and turn right, or west, to 12th. Continue on 12th until you find a view that pleases you. The green space on your right is known as the 12th Avenue Viewpoint.

❻ This spot provides another great view down into the Duwamish River valley. Imagine standing on this spot in the 1850s. Through the forest of Douglas fir, you would have seen one of Seattle's now-vanished ecosystems, the nearly 2,400 acres of the Duwamish River's tideflats. It was a dynamic landscape teeming with fish and fowl, as well as a host of edible invertebrates. At high tide, 10 to 15 feet of water covered the area between Beacon Hill and West Seattle, and at low tide, the water flowed out, leaving an open expanse of mud.

To see evidence from one of Seattle's epic engineering follies, continue south on 12th a couple of blocks until it curves and becomes S Hanford Street.

❼ The wooded valley south of Hanford Street is not natural terrain. What is now a shallow bite out of the side of Beacon was originally solid ground where 12th would have continued south running along what was the western edge of the hill. Eugene Semple's Waterway Company created the chasm

FILLING THE TIDEFLATS

The tideflats began to change in 1895, when former Territorial Governor Eugene Semple's Seattle and Lake Washington Waterway Company started to fill in the watery lowland. Using two specially designed dredges, workers began to suck mud out of what would become the East and West Waterways on either side of Harbor Island. The mud entered a pipe and traveled 2,000 feet to another part of the tideflats—just west of the modern-day Safeco Field—where it was expelled behind bulkheads, or barriers made of piling, brush, and trees.

Semple's goal was to dump enough sediment behind the barriers to make new, usable land, or solid ground, out of what had been unusable terrain. When finished, the new land was two feet above high tide. By 1917, more than 92 percent of the tideflats had been filled, creating about 2,400 acres of new land. Other cities that also made land in a similar mannor include Boston (5,200 acres), San Francisco (more than 3,000 acres), and Manhattan (1,400 acres).

when it attempted to cut a canal through Beacon Hill to connect Elliott Bay with Lake Washington. The so-called south canal would have run through a gorge 300 feet deep and roughly one quarter mile wide. Starting in 1901, workers used hydraulic giants, or water cannons, to cut into the hillside. The excavated material was then sent in pipes to fill in the tideflats directly west of the cut. By late 1904, crews had washed away seven city blocks and dumped enough sediment into the tideflats to create 52 acres of new land. But they would go no farther as the supporters of a north canal—the modern Lake Washington Ship Canal—rallied to kill Semple's project.

The failed attempt at building a south canal would eventually provide the perfect location to build S Columbian Way, which runs up the unnatural cleft and connects Beacon Hill to the Duwamish River valley.

Walk east on Hanford Street to 14th Avenue S.

❽ Note how 14th doesn't align when it crosses Hanford. It most likely has to do with platting, or the official system of dividing land for development. North of Hanford are older plats dating back to 1869—from Edward Hanford's land claim—and south is one as recent as 1924. The jog in the road might have occurred because the later plats had to account for the cut into Beacon Hill made by Semple's crews or because later plats were more accu-

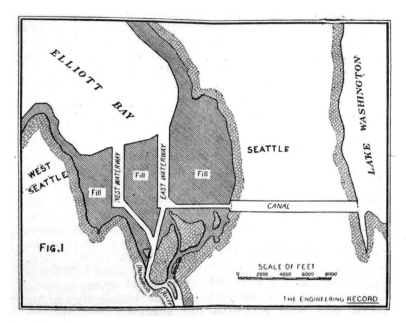

Map of Eugene Semple's proposed south canal through Beacon Hill, 1895

rately mapped, meaning that they corresponded more closely to the city's official grid system. Either way the unusual road alignment is one of the geographic perturbations that make urban history enchanting and sometimes frustrating.

Continue east to Beacon Avenue.

❾ Unlike most streets in Seattle, Beacon Avenue doesn't align with a cardinal direction. Instead, it cuts diagonally across the landscape, following one of the first roads in the county. An early map of Seattle from 1861 shows the "Road from Stelacoom [sic] to Seattle," which ran along Beacon Hill before dropping onto the tideflats and into Seattle. It was one segment of the so-called Military Road that ran from Olympia to Bellingham. South of Seattle on Interstate 5 past Southcenter Mall, exit 151 leads to another section of Military Road.

This is one of the business centers that developed along the Beacon Hill streetcar line, which ran down Beacon Avenue. Trolley service began in the early 1890s, initially ending at Hanford and later extending to Spokane Street. The area around Hanford developed in the 1920s with a tavern, pharmacy, bakery, dentist, and the Three Brothers Dye Works, whose motto was "We Dye to Live." Note the red street lights, which were installed by neighbors in the 1990s.

Turn left, and walk north on Beacon. Veer right on 17th Avenue S at S Forest Street, across the street from the Beacon Hill Branch of the Seattle Public Library.

⑩ Completed in 2004, the library is a fabulous building, with stone elements from the same quarry that provided material for Seattle's downtown Carnegie-funded library. It boasts an open floor plan and invigorating natural light. Plus, it has public restrooms. The streets to your right, or east, cross an area that was originally one of the earliest parts of the Seattle area owned by African American families. In 1869, Boston native George P. Riley and 14 other men and women from Portland, Oregon, formed the Workingmen's Joint Stock Association to pool their resources and purchase real estate. Riley then traveled north to Seattle, which he and other association members had previously passed through after searching for gold in Canada. He paid $2,000 in gold coin for the eastern section of Hanford's original land claim.

Two years later, Riley and the association platted two parcels of land totaling 12 city blocks between what are now 17th and 21st Avenues and Stevens and Lander Streets. Only two members of the group eventually moved to Seattle; Riley's son, George Wright, later built a house on the group's property.

Walk north on 17th Avenue to S Roberto Maestas Festival Street (formerly S Lander Street). Turn left, or west, and walk one block to 16th Avenue S across from the Beacon Hill Light Rail station. Turn right on 16th, and walk north half a block to the large wood frame building on the right.

⑪ Originally built in 1904, the Beacon Hill School became the home of El Centro de la Raza in 1972, when students and staff of the Chicano: English and Adult Basic Education Program at the Duwamish branch of South Seattle Community College peacefully occupied the unoccupied and dilapidated school. El Centro purchased the building in 1999. A social services organization, El Centro focuses on building unity among all races and all ages. The grounds are usually open to the public.

Continue north on 16th Avenue to S Bayview Street, turn left, or west, and walk to 15th Avenue S. Turn right, and walk north one-half block to 2336 15th Avenue S and the home of the Washington State Federation of Garden Clubs.

⑫ Newspaperman, developer, and judge Edward Turner and his wife, Estelle, built the core of what is now the oldest house on Beacon Hill in 1883. After Turner died, Frederick Koepf purchased the home and remodeled it into its present style. But the house was not at its current location. During a regrade of Beacon Avenue around 1907, Koepf moved the house about 100 yards to its present site. In 1977, the Washington State Federation of Garden Clubs acquired the house from the Jefferson Park Ladies Improvement Club, who had bought the building in 1923.

Return south one block on 15th to Beacon Avenue.

⑬ This area around Beacon and 15th, historically known as the "Junction," was the main business center of the hill with a movie house, ten-cent store, tavern, bakery, drugstore, and ice-cream shop. Many of the historic one- and two-story buildings remain, though they may be hidden by modern facades.

Walk north on Beacon Avenue, and turn right at 14th Avenue S. Go two blocks to S Walker Street.

⑭ The brick building on the northeast corner was built in 1928 and occupied around 1930 by the Toyo Grocery. Operated by the Kaminishi family, the grocery served a Japanese American community that had expanded southeast from Japantown, or Nihonmachi, in what is now the International District. During World War II, the Kaminishis were forced to abandon the building and taken to internment camps. In the early 1950s, the Eng family, who were part of a wave of Chinese Americans that moved up to Beacon Hill during and after the war, operated a store in the building. In 1955, George Kaminishi, son of the original store operators, started running the grocery again. He and his wife remained there until 1969.

Walk north two blocks on 14th Avenue S to S Plum Street.

⑮ Across the street (west) is the Beacon Hill Playground, historically the location of Seattle's first reservoir. Built in 1886 and filled with water pumped from Lake Washington, the reservoir proved to be inadequate in supplying water during Seattle's Great Fire of 1889, which ultimately led to Seattleites voting for a new source of water from the Cedar River. The reservoir continued to provide a limited amount of water until it was abandoned in 1912. Fourteen years later, the city parks department filled in the reservoir and converted it to a playfield.

Walk north two blocks on 14th Avenue to S Massachusetts Street. About 100 feet north of Massachusetts on the east side of the street is a two-story building with a circular drive.

🔟 Built in 1904, the building was originally known as Fire Station 13 and served Beacon Hill's main residential and commercial district. Like other stations in the early 1900s, FS 13's fire trucks were horse powered, which created a lot of problems that disappeared with the introduction of motorized trucks. For instance, in 1910 the city Department of Health and Sanitation sent a terse note to the fire chief pointing out that Fire Station 13's manure piles and storage were not up to snuff. Nor were horses the only problem; the station needed to remove the chickens living in the basement. The station closed in 1928, when the fire department built a more centrally located station farther south on Beacon Hill.

Massachusetts Street was also the former home of M. Harwood Young, the man often credited with naming Beacon Hill. He arrived in Seattle in 1889, or possibly 1890 or 1891, and began to invest in real estate and a streetcar trolley on the hill. Young, a Civil War veteran from Boston, supposedly named Beacon Hill after his hometown's famous hill of Brahmins. Historian Rob Ketcherside, however, questions this story. He has found that the earliest reference to Beacon Hill appeared in the *Seattle P-I* on October 10, 1889. In that issue was a letter about renaming Seattle streets by real estate developer Henry Dearborn, whose Beacon Hill was north of the old reservoir at Plum Street. South of Plum would be called Spring Hill, or so proposed Dearborn.

Similar to neighborhoods on other Seattle hills, Beacon illustrates how geography influences development. Its proximity to downtown made it attractive to many, but its physical isolation made it challenging to reach, ultimately resulting in a history of socioeconomic development unique among Seattle neighborhoods.

Walk west on S Massachusetts Street to 12th Avenue, and turn right, or north, to return to Dr. Jose Rizal Park.

Rainier Beach to Columbia City

FROM SLOUGH TO SLOUGH

This walk along Lake Washington highlights the effects of lowering the lake for the ship canal.

DISTANCE	5.5 miles, one-way
STARTING POINT	S Henderson Street and Seward Park Avenue S
ENDING POINT	Near Columbia Branch, Seattle Public Library, 4721 Rainier Avenue S
NOTES	This is a fairly long walk. Some longer stretches are without formal information, but there is plenty to see along the way. You might consider doing it by bike. Restrooms are available at Pritchard Island Beach, Seward Park, and Stan Sayres Memorial Park. The southbound Metro Bus 7 returns you to one block west (Rainier Avenue S and S Henderson Street) of the starting point.

No location on Lake Washington better illustrates the physical and ecological changes that resulted from the construction of the Hiram M. Chittenden Locks and Lake Washington Ship Canal than the shoreline between Rainier Beach and what is now Stan Sayres Memorial Park. The changes

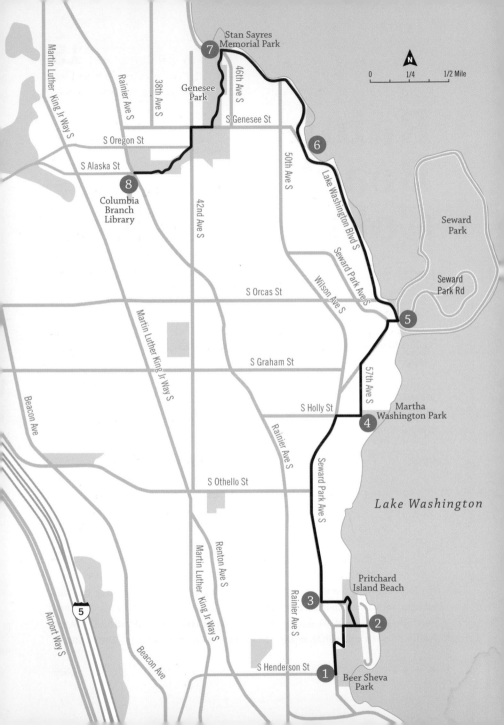

occurred because of the need to lower Lake Washington to the level of Lake Union. If the higher lake hadn't been lowered, two locks would have been necessary: one to connect boats between the lakes and another between Salmon Bay and Puget Sound.

Not until the 20th century did planners agree on the single lock system. The lowering of Lake Washington occurred in 1916 with the connection of the two lakes and Salmon Bay, although the official opening didn't take place until July 4, 1917. (For more information, see Walk 9.)

The ecological repercussions of the canal were dramatic. Before 1916, Lake Washington had a total shoreline of 82 miles and almost 1,100 acres of surrounding wetlands. It drained out through the Black River, which flowed into the Duwamish River and out to Elliott Bay. After the opening of the locks and the subsequent lowering of the lake by nine feet, 99 percent of its wetlands dried up and disappeared, its shoreline shrunk by more than 10 miles, and the Black River was eliminated (the new lake level was lower than its historic outlet). Lock construction also led to Salmon Bay changing from a dynamic ecosystem ruled by tides to a lake controlled by the Army Corps of Engineers. And finally, the loss of the Black River forced migratory fish to find a new way into Lake Washington, instead of following the Duwamish. More than 100 years later, these changes are mostly hidden but clues can be found that illustrate part of the canal story, which is the main focus of this walk.

Start on the east side of the intersection of S Henderson Street and Seward Park Avenue S.

❶ Legend holds that in 1869 Joseph and Catherine Dunlap were traveling by wagon over Beacon Hill when their son George climbed a tree and reported seeing a bucolic valley next to a large lake. The land so enchanted the family that they decided to homestead it. The intersection of Henderson Street and Seward Park Avenue is just east of the Dunlap claim. The land wasn't good for farming because it was not actually solid. Instead, it was a wetland, or slough (originally called Dunlap Slough), that extended northwest across the lowland where Rainier Beach High School now stands.

After the lake dropped, about 74 acres of wetlands remained. The loss of Dunlap Slough, Union Bay bog, Mercer Slough, and Renton marshes left shorelines more vulnerable to severe weather and removed vital habitat for fish and birds. The wetlands were also an important food resource to the

Dunlap Slough to Wetmore Slough,
detail from a USGS map, 1897

Native Americans who lived around the lake. They knew Dunlap Slough as Loon Place, or *dxWwóóqWeeb* in Whulshootseed.

Near the slough was also the terminus of the longest streetcar line in Seattle. It reached here in 1891, with cars leaving for Seattle every 45 minutes. The ride to town cost a dime. By 1896, the line extended to Renton. As was true for other trolley lines that ended at the lake, including ones terminating at Leschi and Madison Park, the Rainier Beach trolley played a key role in settlement by opening access to outlying areas.

One person who took advantage of the growing community was Clarence D. Hillman. In 1905, he platted the land north of Dunlap Slough as Atlantic City. To entice buyers, he said he would preserve part of the property as a public park. After selling several parcels, however, Hillman, who had a reputation as not the most honest of chaps, replatted the land, eliminating the park. Several buyers sued and the court declared that the park had to remain. In 1978, the city changed the name of Hillman's Atlantic City Park to Beer Sheva Park to honor Seattle's sister city in Israel.

The most recent change to the park began in 2014, with a restoration project on Mapes Creek (Henry and Eva Jane Mapes platted land near here in 1909), which had flowed into the slough. Crews moved the creek out of a pipe and into a stream channel, with the goal of improving habitat for juvenile Chinook salmon, which historically would have thrived in or near the slough.

Walk north on Seward Park Avenue S, turn right, or east, on Wabash Avenue S, which becomes 55th Avenue S. Walk north to S Cloverdale Street, turn right, and walk to Island Drive S.

➋ The dip you crossed was formerly part of Dunlap Slough. Before 1916, the wetland made the peninsula where you now stand into an island, known to Native people as *TlúTlatSas* (small island) and to settlers as

WETLAND, SLOUGH, BOG, OR MARSH?

Wetland is the generic term for land that is wet for some period of time.

Slough, at least in the West, generally refers to a quiet backwater of a larger body of water.

Bogs are characterized by wet, spongy soil dominated by peat moss.

Marshes are wetlands frequently or continually inundated with nutrient-rich water.

Young's Island, after its first owner Andrew B. Young, an early druggist in the city. Young sold the island in 1900 to Alfred J. Pritchard, who built a house and spanned the gap to the island with a small footbridge. When the lake dropped and the slough drained, Pritchard tried to cash in on the newly created property. His advertisements in the *Seattle Times* promoted "some of the richest tracts of land anywhere about Seattle." All buyers had to do was pay $16 down with monthly payments of $16, interest included.

Return west on Cloverdale from Island Drive, walk past Park Drive S, and look for a gravel path on the right, which will take you north through the now forested former wetland. (The path is dry.) Follow the path through to a parking lot at Pritchard Island Beach. Enjoy the green space, and then exit the park on S Grattan Street, and walk west to Seward Park Avenue S. Turn right, and walk north. This section (1.25 miles to the next turn at S Holly Street) has little commentary but many remarkable homes and yards. Here are a few things to note along the way. (Numbered stop 3 denotes right turn on Seward Park Avenue.)

❸ There are a high number of houses built with local sandstone and different styles of brick or a combination of the two. Around the 7700 block of Seward Park, look for old lampposts (somewhat hidden by vegetation) with curious metal fish (about three inches tall) atop them.

A block or so north is Wildwood Lane. In the early 1900s, a walkway connected Wildwood and Matthiesen Station on the Rainier Avenue street trolley to Twin Firs resort, the former lakeside home of John Matthiesen, who purchased 80 acres along the lake. Visitors, who would stay for weeks at a time in the summer, could either lodge in the house or set up a tent on the grounds.

North of Othello Street on Seward Park Avenue, the neighborhood is known as Brighton Beach. Everett and Mary Smith platted the property in 1890, naming it for the beach resort in England. The Smiths named their estate Morningside and built a greenhouse, boathouse, and barn to go with their home. Within the plat was Wilson Avenue, which honored John Wilson, who originally owned the land. Part of Wilson Avenue became Seward Park Avenue.

Turn right at S Holly Street, and descend east to the end of the road at Martha Washington Park.

❹ The Seattle School District purchased this land—the Smith's Morningside estate—in 1919 for the Girls Parental School. Created to provide education for girls who were wards of the Juvenile Court of King County, the school included classes on reading, writing, and arithmetic, along with lessons in skills such as serving, laundry work, and darning. Up to 90 girls could be housed in a brick two-story building, which became known as the Martha Washington School for Girls in 1931. It closed as a residential school in 1965 and was demolished in 1989.

Walk north on 57th Avenue S to Seward Park Avenue S, turn right, or east, and continue to S Juneau Street. Turn right, and walk one block to Lake Washington Boulevard S and the entrance to Seward Park. Several trails wind through the park, and a paved 2.5-mile road circumnavigates it.

❺ Seward Park, or *squbáqst* (noses) as the Native people knew it, and Bailey Peninsula, as it was known until 1911, feature some of the rare unlogged, or at least very lightly logged, forest in Seattle. One famous tree is the city's largest Douglas fir, a seven-foot-diameter giant estimated to be at least 500 years old. The park also contains good habitat for native bigleaf maple, madrona, Garry oak, and poison oak, which is not a true oak but is in the cashew family. Landowner Philip Ritz, who paid $188.44 for 151 acres in 1868, did not live in the area, which may account for the minimal logging.

Named for William Bailey (who bought Ritz's property for $26,000 in 1889), the peninsula was not always so well connected to the mainland. According to Everett and Mary Smith's son Harold, the peninsula could become an island in winter, when additional water could raise the lake level as much as seven feet over the summer low. After 1916, the lake was too low to

GARRY OAK

What makes Martha Washington Park particularly interesting is its unique ecosystem, which historically consisted of Garry oaks. Washington State's lone native oak species appears to have been restricted in Seattle to the area between Pritchard Island and Seward Park, with outlier specimens at what was Oak Lake, modern home of Oak Tree Village. More common south of Tacoma, Garry oaks prefer sunny, open, well-drained sites, especially prairies. The biggest one at Martha Washington had a 14-foot circumference and was 75 feet tall until it fell in the winter of 1987. At present, nine large oaks and several saplings grow in the park between the main lawn and a dirt path along the shoreline. (The big trees along 57th are sycamore maples; just west are several elms.)

Why oaks grew at this location is unclear. We know that Native people who harvested acorns on the Tacoma prairies kept out shrubs and Douglas firs by regularly setting fires. One possibility is that the area south of Seward, formerly known as Clark's Prairie (Edward A. Clark staked a claim on the property in April 1852), had been colonized by oaks, and Native people managed the land to protect the trees and their acorns. The best evidence for this is a General Land Office survey in 1861, which listed two "deadenings," or fire-charred locations, for Clark's Prairie. (Despite the street name Holly, no holly is native to this area.)

cover the isthmus. The peninsula became known as Seward Park after the city exercised its right of eminent domain and acquired the land through condemnation for $322,020 in 1910.

Continue north on Lake Washington Boulevard S for a little under two miles to 46th Avenue S and Stan Sayres Memorial Park and the Mount Baker Rowing and Sailing Center. Here are few things to consider as you walk along. (Numbered stop 6 indicates the midpoint between Seward and Sayres Parks.)

6 Many sections of the path along the road above the lake are roughly equal in elevation to the historic level of Lake Washington (about nine feet higher) before it dropped in 1916.

In the 1930s, Donald E. Frederick, cofounder of Frederick & Nelson Department Store, one of Seattle's great institutions, created a bird sanctuary in the bay north of Seward Park. Each year Frederick would pay for tons of grain to be distributed to waterfowl. He told a *Seattle Times* reporter that he had been motivated to do so because he had "shot so many ducks in his life he thought he should do something to make up for it." By the time he died in 1937, the sanctuary attracted thousands of birds and more than a thousand weekend bird-watchers, which did not necessarily please the neighbors.

When you reach Lakewood Moorage, you may not be able to tell, but there is a small island (with several low structures on it) in the bay. Ohler Island (located where stop 6 appears on the map) emerged after the 1916 lake lowering. It first appeared on a map in 1920 and was linked to the mainland in 1952.

Along this stretch of the lake, you will see to your left, or west, that the land rises steeply, gaining more than 150 feet in a few blocks. If you were to look at a map depicting Seattle's subsurface geology, you would discover that an unusual rock makes up these hills. Unlike most Seattle hills, such as Queen Anne and Capitol, which are made of relatively soft sediments deposited during the last ice age, these hills consist of a hard sandstone deposited between 23 and 28 million years ago. Known as the Blakeley Formation, it occurs around Seward Park and at Alki Point in West Seattle. The northern extent of the hills along the lake marks the northern extent of the Blakeley.

At Stan Sayres Memorial Park, cross Lake Washington Boulevard to a gravel path that goes west into Genesee Park. *Be careful: cars tend to speed through this area.*

❼ Sayres Park was named for a famous hydroplane racer in the 1940s and '50s. This is the main dock for Seattle's annual Seafair hydroplane races.

In 1870, Seymour Wetmore homesteaded the area around what became known as Wetmore Slough, a cattail- and tule-filled wetland that stretched south and west past Genesee Street almost to Rainier Avenue. To cross the slough, travelers went over a wooden trestle bridge. The slough drained, and for the most part disappeared, after the lake dropped in 1916, but local residents complained that it was a source of noxious odors and an incubator for mosquitoes. In 1937, construction crews began to replace the old trestle with fill excavated from the lake. Six years later, the city decided to convert the area to a "sanitary fill," which generated a new round of complaints, this time about dog-size rats and aromas more malodorous than ever. The dump finally closed in the late '60s.

SEATTLE FAULT

The Seattle Fault is a zone of weakness that runs underground from Issaquah below the two sports stadiums to Bainbridge Island. Over the past 10 to 15 million years, tectonic movement has squeezed the rocks along the fault, thrusting those on the south side, including the Blakeley, up several thousand feet. In this area, and at Alki Point in West Seattle, those rocks have pierced the surface and created high spots, made of rock hard enough that it resisted erosion during the last ice age.

The last major movement, or uplift, along the Seattle Fault occurred 1,100 years ago. During that earthquake, the ground rose 20 feet. The shaking also created a small tsunami in Puget Sound; sent three groves of trees landsliding into Lake Washington, where they still stand upright on the bottom of the lake; and caused rock slides on the Olympic Peninsula that dammed streams and made lakes.

Scientists first reported on the Seattle Fault in December 1992. Since then, they have found several more strands of the fault and discovered that it has moved many times. Because the fault zone is so close to the surface—less than 10 miles below Seattle—geologists fear that when it next moves it will cause catastrophic damage in the region.

Former territorial governor and United States Senator Watson C. Squire first used the name Genesee on a 1904 plat of land he owned. He appears to have been inspired by his upbringing in upstate New York—Genesee comes from a Seneca Indian word meaning "beautiful valley."

Follow the gravel path south as it runs along the buried dump. When you reach S Genesee Street, turn right, or west, walk to 42nd Avenue S, and turn left. Walk to S Conover Way, where a path leads west. Follow the path as it winds to the left of a small playground to S Alaska Street. Turn right, and walk to Rainier Avenue S. Across the street is a bus stop for the southbound Metro Bus route 7 (in front of the library), which will take you back to the beginning of the route.

❽ In 1889, James K. Edmiston (who was pardoned by Washington's governor in 1911 after being on the lam for 17 years because of financial malfeasance) began the Rainier Avenue Electric Railway to bring people

Wetmore Slough Bridge, 1913

from downtown Seattle out to an area he was getting ready to develop. He named the new townsite Columbia and platted streets with names honoring famed explorers Americus Vespucci, Ferdinand Magellan, and Henry Hudson. The first lots sold in 1891, and by 1893 enough people lived in the area for residents to establish Columbia City. The City of Seattle annexed Columbia City in 1907.

Behind the Columbia Branch library (built in 1915 with funds provided by Andrew Carnegie) on Rainier Avenue S is one final connection to Wetmore Slough. What is now Columbia Park was once a riparian corridor. Historically, Hitt's Creek flowed through a 40-foot-deep ravine that ran behind the library. The creek started a few blocks south as a spring at Hitt's Hill (now a city park) and continued to Wetmore Slough. (Thomas Gabriel Hitt owned Hitt Fireworks Company.) A demand by residents for a more accessible public space led the Seattle Parks Department to put the creek in a pipe and fill in the ravine in the mid-1920s with more than 84,000 cubic yards of garbage and other debris.

Although Columbia City is nearly a mile from Lake Washington, some local promoters envisioned it as a "seaport town." Hoping to take advantage of the new connection to saltwater, the boosters' 1928 plan called for dredging a 200-foot-wide, 2,000-foot-long canal up the old Wetmore Slough. According to dredging advocate Joseph Shepherd, the canal would create "the best small boat haven on Lake Washington." Like so many other fantastic ideas in Seattle—the south canal through Beacon Hill, tunnels under Lake Washington, filling in Lake Union—seaport Columbia was a better idea than actual project.

Delridge and Pigeon Point

THE LESSER-KNOWN SIDE
OF WEST SEATTLE

After a short walk up Longfellow Creek, this route leads over to two less-explored but interesting neighborhoods.

DISTANCE	4.4 miles
START/END	Cul-de-sac just east of SW Yancy Street and 28th Avenue SW
NOTES	This is a fairly long walk that has some stretches without formal information, but there is plenty to see along the way. The walk has several long flights of stairs, the longest of which ascends 135 steps. Restrooms are sparse but should be available at Delridge Community Center and South Seattle College. If you are feeling tired halfway through, Metro Bus route 125 runs from South Seattle College to within a block or two of the starting point.

Often overlooked by people headed to West Seattle, this quiet dell between two ridges was settled by William Heebner. In 1853, he filed a claim for what became known as Young's Cove, a tideflat that used to extend south of the modern-day West Seattle Bridge into the Nucor Steel plant property. There is no known date of or origin for the first use of the name Young's Cove, but

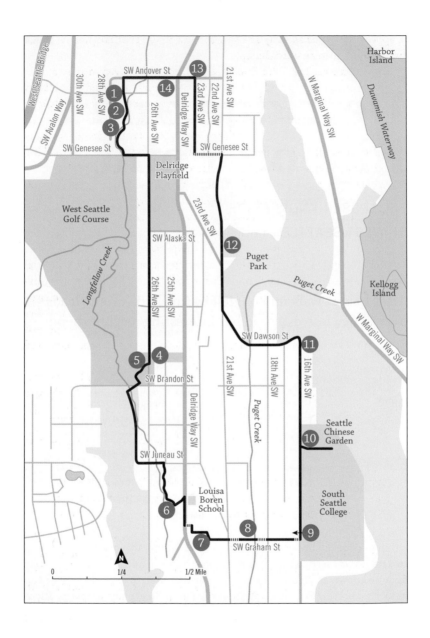

it appears on maps as early as 1894, the same year that Longfellow Creek first shows up on an official map.

Eight years earlier, John Enoch Longfellow had moved into what was called Humphry, or Humphry's Settlement, though again no one knows who Humphry was. Longfellow started a logging company and eventually became a councilman in West Seattle. Change came again in 1905 when William Piggott and Elliot M. Wilson opened the Seattle Steel Company (now Nucor Steel) and named the area Youngstown, after the steel-making town in Ohio where both had formerly lived.

As the steel plant prospered, Youngstown grew with the addition of workers, many of whom were immigrants, including Greeks, Italians, and Russians. For some time the area was known as Poverty Gulch and Garlic Gulch. Above the lowland, Pigeon Point was populated by Scandinavians. By the late 1930s, steel was no longer as important to the community as it had been, and residents decided they wanted to project a less industrial image. They pushed to change the name to Dell Ridge. On May 13, 1940, the Seattle City Council passed an ordinance creating the new name Delridge.

More recently, Delridge has been transformed again as residents have worked to restore Longfellow Creek. They have removed garbage, improved habitat for native plants and animals, created a signed trail, and increased public awareness of and access to the creek.

East of Longfellow Creek is another intriguing part of West Seattle, the long land wrinkle of Puget Ridge and Puget Creek that joins north into Pigeon Point. Logged and later sold or donated by its landowner, Puget Mill Company, it is an unusual and less-visited part of West Seattle.

This walk starts out in Longfellow Creek, leaves the creek to explore the neighborhood to the east, and returns via the site of a historic stairway.

Start on the east side of the intersection of SW Yancy Street and 28th Avenue SW, where Yancy dead-ends at a cul-de-sac. This is the beginning of the Longfellow Creek Legacy Trail, which is marked by two decorated metal columns.

❶ Longfellow Creek historically ended about a block north of Yancy in the southern end of Young's Cove. It now drops into a 90-inch-diameter pipe and runs underground for 3,257 feet into the Duwamish West Waterway. The Native name for the mouth of the creek (t7áWee) has been translated as both smelt and trout, the latter of which inhabited the creek. Smelt are small fish that spawn in the intertidal zone and would have used the tidally influenced

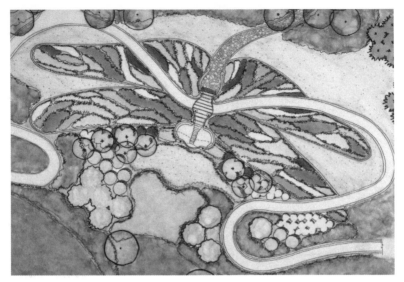

Lorna Jordan's plan of her Dragonfly Garden

Young's Cove. (Because the creek now drains into Elliott Bay, saltwater fish such as flounder occasionally make it up the pipe to the creek.)

Walk upstream, or south, on the Legacy Trail path, which soon forks. The main trail goes left, but take the short spur to the right that leads up to a unique garden and artwork.

❷ Artist Lorna Jordan designed the Dragonfly Pavilion so that it "appears ready to take flight—offering vistas of the watershed's rolling topography." The space consists of the giant dragonfly, plant beds, a terrazzo mosaic, and earthworks. What may not be obvious from the ground is that the plant beds are laid out in the shape of even more massive, outstretched dragonfly wings.

Return to the main trail, turn right, and continue upstream. Stay right as the trail forks, and in about 100 yards you will pass over and through a bridge.

❸ The second of Lorna Jordan's large art projects along the creek is her Salmon Bone Bridge, which was built to accommodate the creek at flood stage, as well as to provide a more visceral experience of the fish that used to regularly, and now less often, swim up Longfellow. Note the herringbone

Salmon Bone Bridge

pattern of the recycled cedar timbers and the metal pipe, which references the nearby steel plant. Farther up the creek, where the water flows under a roadway, are stream improvements designed to enhance salmon habitat.

At present, chum and coho salmon spawn in the creek, though they face many challenges. The first is entering the creek via the screened pipe that drains into the Duwamish West Waterway. Next they must swim sixth-tenths of a mile in darkness before emerging into the creek's open water. Perhaps their greatest challenge is the toxic stew of heavy metals, motor oil, fertilizers, and other pollutants that runs off streets and into the creek. Coho are particularly susceptible to these chemical hazards because they return to spawn when the creek is running at higher water and carrying the most storm water–derived contaminants.

Research shows that this has led to abnormally high pre-spawn mor-tality. Compared with non-urban creeks where the mortality is as low as 1 percent, Longfellow Creek has seen death rates of 60 to 100 percent. This is probably the main contributor to the drop in returning coho, which ran as high as 300 to 400 in the 1990s but now number in the dozens. Most of the salmon that do return are probably not native to Longfellow but are hatchery fish or fish born in another part of the Duwamish River's drainage area. Even if the salmon do survive, they can't make it very far up the creek; a culvert in the West Seattle Golf Course, about a quarter mile upstream, prevents the fish from continuing toward the creek's headwaters.

Continue up the main trail, past a stairway on your left, and under a roadway. When the trail forks, veer left to a flight of steps that leads up to SW Genesee Street. Ascend them, turn left on Genesee, walk to 26th Avenue SW, and turn right. For about three-quarters of a mile, you will be away from the creek. This is a good section along which to notice the difference between the modest homes in this historic working-class neighborhood and the larger, more modern homes later in the walk. Continue south on 26th Avenue until you reach two small parks at Puget Boulevard SW.

❹ 26th Avenue and the streets east to 23rd were developed by the Puget Mill Company in 1918 as the working-class Cottage Grove neighborhood. Advertisements in the *Seattle Times* promoted the rich soil, easy access to the steelworks, a flour mill, and shipyards, and promised that Puget Mill would provide wood for those who wanted to build their own home. "Wives are helping, and keenly enjoy the part they play with hammer and saw," according to an advertisement.

From a geological point of view, the valley you are walking in is relatively unusual in Seattle. Most hills in the city consist of sediment deposited during the glacial advance of the last ice age. (For more information, see Walk 12). In contrast, the sediments in the Longfellow Creek valley were deposited as the glacier retreated, or melted, back to the north. Streams washing out of the receding glacier's mouth flowed south in the low elevation areas between the hills or cut their own channels and deposited layers of sand, silt, and gravel. Also in this valley are finer-grained sediments carried by the streams into large lakes that covered much of the Puget lowland after glacial retreat. Eventually though, the ice retreated—at a rate of about 1,100 feet per year—far enough north to allow the lakes to drain into the Strait of Juan de Fuca.

Enter Greg Davis Park on the west side of 26th Avenue, about one half block past Puget Boulevard. The main entrance consists of a kiosk near several boulders.

❺ Originally owned by the Puget Mill Company and later by the City of Seattle as part of the West Seattle Golf Course, Greg Davis Park is an outgrowth of community work beginning in the 1990s. Volunteers developed plans for the landscape, removed nonnative species, and planted more than 66,000 natives. The park honors Greg Davis and his commitment to the Delridge neighborhood and to the establishment of a place that he hoped would include "green meadows and trees that people can enjoy." He died in 1993.

Also note the poetry carved into the boulders near the kiosk. The lines are from "October's Party," written in 1879 by New York–born poet George Cooper. (I am not sure why the poem is dated 1902.) Across the street is Cottage Grove Park, named after the old Puget Mill development.

To return to the creek, follow the trail that heads south from the kiosk and wraps around the west side of the grassy area. The trail takes you past a small information sign to SW Brandon Street. Cross the road, pass between two decorated metal columns, and follow the trail, which curves around to a wooden bridge. Cross the bridge, turn left, and stay on the main trail as it runs along the creek under alder trees. After the trail reaches a more open area, continue south until it ends at a power substation. Turn left at the station on SW Juneau Street, and walk east to 25th Avenue SW. Turn right onto the Longfellow Legacy Trail, and follow it to the second wooden bridge/boardwalk. To the right is a clearing and a beaver pond.

Ⓖ You may not be able to discern it amid the vegetation, but there are a beaver dam and lodge in this open space. As occurred on creeks across Seattle, the Longfellow beavers arrived on their own, found suitable habitat (water and food), and built a colony. A typical family consists of adults, yearlings, and kits. Once they reach sexual maturity, beavers go in search of a new home, in this case, one of our local streams. The scientific name for beaver, *Castor canadensis*, refers to the *castoreum*, musk-secreting glands. It is not the source of castor oil, which comes from a tropical plant.

Shortly beyond the bridge, the trail forks. Turn left, and follow the trail up to the street, Delridge Way SW. At this point, the route leaves the creek to explore the ridges to the east. Cross Delridge Way at the crosswalk, which takes you to the Louisa Boren School. Turn right, and walk south on Delridge, next to the school's parking lot. At the car entrance to the lot, turn left over to a flight of stairs. Ascend them, and turn right along the fence of a baseball field. Walk south around the fence, turn left, and walk east across the field toward a telephone pole and a yellow metal guard rail. Behind, or east of the pole, is a staircase that ascends SW Graham Street (no street exists here, only the

Beaver

staircase). This is the first of four flights of stairs (129 up, 72 down, 99 up, and another 50 up) that will take you over Puget Ridge to South Seattle College.

❼ Take a break before you begin your climb to consider the geology of the hill you are about to ascend. Like the valley below, it is unusual; in this case, the sides consist of sediments deposited *before* the ice entered Seattle during the last ice age, most likely prior to 60,000 years ago. The layers are often very dense because they have been compressed and consolidated under the weight of the glacier that subsequently passed over them. This compaction process made the rocks more resistant to erosion, which geologists have hypothesized could contribute to why Puget Ridge has such steep sides.

At the top of the first flight of stairs, continue east on SW Graham Street across 21st Avenue SW to a staircase down into the ravine of Puget Creek. Stop at the bottom.

❽ The headwaters for Puget Creek are about one-half mile south in a wooded wetland at Sanislo Elementary School. From the school, the creek flows for a little under two miles to the Duwamish River. As happened with the vast majority of Seattle's waterways, Puget Creek suffered from decades of neglect and abuse. Longtime residents remember hunting crawdads in the creek, which flowed year-round with deep pools where bathers could cool off in the summer. But when the wetland at the creek's headwaters was paved over, the flow became more intermittent.

BEAVERS IN SEATTLE

No one knows exactly how many beavers are in Seattle, but based on the number of beaver colonies on urban creeks, 500 would not be unrealistic. And researchers expect that number to increase. Seattle is an ideal place for North America's largest rodent because it has few predators, mild winters, and a nearly unlimited food supply of fast-growing vegetation. In addition, a ban on body-gripping traps in 2001 has reduced the number of trapped beavers from a statewide average of 6,000 per year to under 1,000.

Our local beavers also benefit from a paradigm shift in beaver management, as residents and land managers realize that beavers are economically and ecologically beneficial. The main economic benefit is that it is far cheaper in the long run to manage for beavers than to remove them over and over again; if the habitat is right, it is nearly impossible to keep them away. Ecological benefits of the beavers' dam building include creating larger and more varied wildlife habitat, recharging groundwater, slowing down floodwaters, and reducing stream sediment load. A recent study also shows that beaver-created wetlands dramatically increase the number and diversity of fish in a stream ecosystem.

Not everyone views beavers as beneficial. Their dam building can flood homes, block culverts, and kill valuable trees. In some cases, the most plausible solution is nonlethal management, such as trapping, which has led to a novel endeavor in Snohomish County. The Sky Beaver Project is taking nuisance beavers and returning them to mountain habitat (live relocation only occurs because of the cooperation of the Tulalip Tribes), which has the added benefit of reducing the impacts of climate change. Because beaver dams aid in water storage and aquifer recharge, they can substitute for the predicted dwindling snowpack, and help increase the amount of available water. The most successful nonlethal approach in terms of cost, time, and long-term benefits is the use of pond-leveling devices, or pipes that allow water to flow through a dam, thus limiting flooding.

In recent years, neighborhood residents have rallied to protect and restore the creek. They stopped a proposed development in the ravine; have removed invasives, such as Himalayan blackberry, English ivy, and holly; and have worked with neighbors to return their yards to a more native environment. They are also working with the Duwamish Tribe at the lower end of Puget Creek, where it drains into the Duwamish River.

Ascend out of the ravine, cross 18th Avenue SW, continue east on SW Graham Street, and climb a final staircase to 16th Avenue SW. South Seattle College is across the street. Turn left, or north, on 16th Avenue SW. (If need be, you can find stops for a north-bound Metro Bus 125 across the street both north and south on 16th.)

❾ Soon you will pass the Duwamish Cohousing project on the west side of the street, which opened in 2000. It contains 20 small dwellings, plus 3 larger dwellings, and a Common House for gatherings and meals. The buildings' small footprint protects a wetland and intermittent stream.

A short way north is a crosswalk that is probably the best place to cross 16th Avenue to the east side. Continue north to the north entrance to South Seattle College Campus, its arboretum, and the Seattle Chinese Garden.

❿ Within the campus are two small gardens well worth exploring. Opened in 2011, the Seattle Chinese Garden is a cooperative project with Chongqing, Seattle's sister city in China, to create a Sichuan-style garden. Combining beauty and harmony, yin and yang, Sichuan gardens allow for both civic celebration and quiet contemplation. Sections within the 4.6-acre Seattle garden include the Knowing the Spring Courtyard, a stunning tree peony garden, and the Song Mei Pavilion, as well as a surprising peek-a-boo view over the trees to downtown Seattle.

Adjacent to the garden is the arboretum, which students established in 1978. It includes perhaps the best conifer collection in the area, particularly the Coenosium Rock Garden and the Milton Sutton Conifer Garden, as well as sensory, shade, and native gardens. More than 100 conifer varieties from around the world are a riot of texture, size, shape, and color. The arboretum also offers another view toward downtown Seattle. Both viewpoints are better in winter when there aren't leaves on the trees.

Continue north on 16th Avenue SW. You will want to be on the left, or west, side of the street—the sidewalk on the east side disappears when the road makes a sharp turn to the left and descends into a valley, where it becomes SW Dawson Street. (It's about a third of a mile from stop 10 to stop 11.) Stop just before the road turns.

⓫ The road cannot go straight because of the steep ravine to the north. This green space is part of the West Duwamish Greenbelt, the longest continuously

STAIRWAYS OF SEATTLE

Seattle has more than 650 stairways, making it one of the most stair-studded cities in the country. According to Jake and Cathy Jaramillo's *Seattle Stairway Walks*, we have about the same number as San Francisco but lose out to Pittsburgh for grand champion. The city's longest, 338 stairs, is on Howe Street on the west side of Capitol Hill, and its oldest, built in 1904, is the 42 steps that connect the two lanes of Ward Street where it intersects Warren Avenue N on the southeast slope of Queen Anne Hill.

We have so many stairs, of course, because of our glacial past and the ridges and troughs carved by the 3,000-foot-thick sheet of ice that once covered the landscape. Some stairways even reflect this recent geology. Look for ones where the steps are uneven or tilted, which indicates that the ground has moved since the stairway was built. These tilted stairways tend to be in areas prone to landslides.

Although the vast majority of stairways are made from concrete, there are also ones built from timber, metal, brick, granite, and old trolley-car track slabs. These less durable ones are slowly being replaced by the city, as are the old handrails made of wood and old trolley-car rails.

---

connected forest in the city. The dominant bigleaf maple, black cotton-wood, and red alder—all native—grow in the greenbelt for two reasons. The steep slopes along the west side of the Duwamish River were and still are prone to landslides. In an unstable environment like this, the first trees to move in are generally alders and maples, which grow quickly in the open habitat. Second, when the region's dominant, original forest of Douglas fir, western red cedar, and western hemlock was logged out, the seed source for future generations of conifers disappeared, which further allowed the pioneer trees to take over.

Most of the area you have been walking along since you left Longfellow Creek was owned by the Puget Mill Company. In 1911, it proposed to donate a 160-foot-wide right-of-way for a boulevard that would run from the Duwamish River up and over Puget Ridge almost to the present-day golf course. Although the parks department made plans to build the road, it was never completed. Puget Mill also donated 20 acres for a property to be called Puget Park.

It is one-half mile to the next stop. Continue on SW Dawson Street as it drops into a valley and then ascends the other side, where it veers into 21st Avenue SW. Continue straight, or north, on 21st, and note the sign on the east side of the road for the West Duwamish Greenbelt. When the road forks, stay right on 21st, and cross at the crosswalk to the east side of the road.

⑫ You have now entered the Pigeon Point neighborhood. The origin of the term *Pigeon* is not known. The local band-tailed pigeon could have nested in the area and/or rock doves (aka pigeons) could have become abundant feeding on material that spilled out of a large grain elevator north of the point. In about a hundred yards, a path leads to the east into the greenbelt. It is a delightful area to explore.

The area east of the road has a curious history. In 1941, the US Government began acquiring property on the ridge as a transmitter site for the Alaska Communications System, which was originally known as the Washington Alaska Military Cable and Telegraph System (WAMCATS). It consisted of 1,497 miles of telegraph wires and 2,128 miles of oceanic cable linking Alaska to Seattle and the rest of the United States. The site eventually totaled 44 acres and included several tuning huts, housing, a five-car garage, and a concrete transmitter building, which was built underground so it would be less vulnerable to attack. In 1958, the University of Washington acquired the property and began to use it for antenna and radio science research, cosmic ray studies, and oncology experiments.

Of particular interest to oncology researcher E. Donnall Thomas was the subterranean transmitter building where he planned to work with dogs that had lymphoma. He needed the safety of a buried building to conduct radiation studies that would help him understand why bone-marrow transplants typically failed. Thomas's work began with dogs and continued with humans, who were irradiated and then transferred from Puget Ridge across town to a hospital. The work was so successful that Dr. Thomas won the Nobel Prize for Physiology or Medicine in 1990 for his work on bone-marrow transplantation research.

The University of Washington vacated the facility in 1985, and Seattle Parks and Seattle Schools acquired it in 1998. The parking lot of the elementary school was built directly atop the underground bunker, which was sealed shut. Recently, a variety of groups have worked to restore the site and many other parts of the greenbelt.

Continue north on 21st Avenue SW until SW Genesee Street, turn left, or west, and walk over to two flights of stairs descending toward Delridge. This is the site of the historic stairway mentioned at the beginning of the walk. Two schools served this area: one along the Duwamish River and one in Youngstown (now the Youngstown Cultural Arts Center). To carry messages between the two, boys would use stairways at this location and one on the east side of Pigeon Point. The west side stairs have since been rebuilt. Descend the stairs, turn right on 23rd Avenue SW, and walk north to SW Andover Street. (Total stairs you descend is 153.)

⑬ On the northeast corner is a building that began life as the Bayview Congregational Church in 1916. Also known as the Mayflower Church, in 1953 it became the home offices for Local 1208, United Steelworkers of America (CIO). The union totaled about 1,000 workers from the Bethlehem Pacific Steel Corporation at the bottom of the hill.

Across the street to the west is the former home of the Youngstown Corps of the Salvation Army. Started by Swedish immigrants in the 1920s, the Salvation Army hosted a Sunday school and a variety of groups such as Boy Scouts and Girl Scouts. Barbara Iacolucci, who grew up in the neighborhood, said the "Salvation Army was a place you could go and feel comfortable if you couldn't dress up, if you didn't have suits and ties and things. You were made welcome and made to feel comfortable there."

Walk west down SW Andover Street to Delridge Way SW.

⑭ Known as the Gulch, the lowland around Delridge Way was the commercial district of Youngstown with a grocery store, meat market, drugstore, and fresh fruit and vegetable stands. Nearby was the neighborhood school, now restored and converted into the Youngstown Cultural Arts Center, one block south of here. More notorious were the taverns, whorehouse, and street gangs, including the "east side of the creek" gang and the "cross the creek" gang.

For many decades, Delridge was not considered the best neighborhood in Seattle, but like many parts of the city it has been reinvigorated with new development, both economically and ecologically. Delridge's residents though have not forgotten their past, which they have honored with displays in the arts center. At a time when many cities show off their prestigious neighborhoods and overlook the vibrant histories of the working-class parts of town, Delridge shows that there is another approach to civic pride.

Follow Andover back to 28th Avenue SW and the beginning of the walk.

West Seattle

OLD GROWTH AND ALKI POINT

Trek through the great forest of Schmitz Preserve Park, get unparalleled views out to Puget Sound, stroll along the water, and end by passing the birthplace of Seattle.

DISTANCE	4.4 miles
START/END	Alki Playground and Whale Tail Park
NOTES	The walk traverses a one-third mile dirt path in Schmitz Preserve Park. The path can be muddy and requires crossing a narrow creek (two feet wide) on flat rocks. The walk has a few short steep sections up the Schmitz Preserve Park trail and one long descent on a sidewalk. Public restrooms are available near the beginning of the walk, but that's about it.

Seattle's standard founding story begins on November 13, 1851, when the schooner *Exact* dropped off the 22 members of the Denny Party on a prominent point of land jutting out into Puget Sound. Inhabited for thousands of years by indigenous people, the point had been named Point Roberts in 1841 by Charles Wilkes's United States Exploring Expedition (there were four people named Roberts on the expedition), but that name would not survive the settlers' ambitions, and the landing spot would eventually become known as Alki Point.

Despite the abundant assistance provided by the Native residents, who knew of Alki as *sbaqWábaqs*, or Prairie Point, the early settlers did not stay long, and by early 1852 most had moved across Elliott Bay to what is now

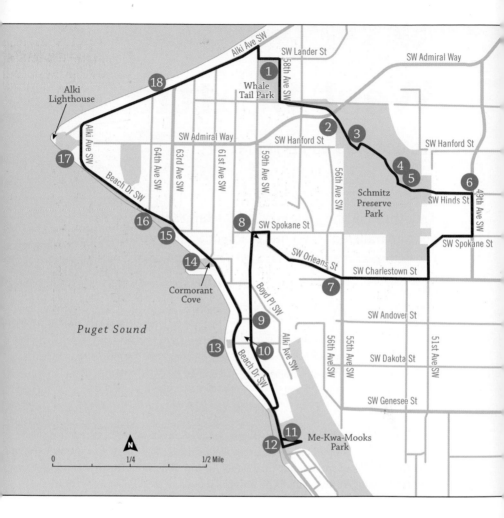

Pioneer Square. Soon, only Charles Terry remained. An ambitious man, he named the area New York and opened a store. In the first edition of Washington Territory's first paper, *The Columbian*, he advertised his "well known stand in the town of New York, on Puget's Sound." But he, too, would abandon the peninsula (and the name New York, which he changed to Alki in 1853) and move to the new town of Seattle. Next to attempt to settle the

Entrance to Schmitz Park, 1911

point was Doc Maynard, one of Seattle's early colorful characters. When his attempts at farming failed, he sold his land in 1868, and Alki Point was more or less forsaken for the next several decades.

Alki eventually developed as a resort community; by 1901, there were perhaps 200 full-time residents and 3,000 who summered on the point. Six years later, Seattle would officially annex West Seattle and incorporate it into the city. More development followed as a trolley reached Alki, a school opened, and the rest of West Seattle started to grow.

Start at 58th Avenue SW and SW Lander Street, at the northeast corner of the park.

1 In 1908, Ferdinand and Emma Schmitz gave 30 acres of forested land to the city. They would eventually donate more. Their lands, combined with other purchases, led to the creation of the modern 53-acre Schmitz Preserve Park. Ferdinand had arrived in Seattle in 1887 and made his fortune in real estate. He was also on the Board of Park Commissioners, which in 1908 was implementing John Charles Olmsted's plans for Seattle Parks. Olmsted described the Schmitz property as a "magnificent natural park . . . unequalled in the Northwest." To provide accessibility, he designed a broad boulevard that took people about one-half mile into the forested terrain.

> Walk south on 58th Avenue, and turn left, or east, at the dead-end sign. You are now on Schmitz Boulevard (don't take SW Stevens), the original, Olmsted-designed park entrance road. Walk through the new entrance and under the tall trees until a bit past the Admiral Way bridge, which passes over the ravine.

❷ For such a small park, Schmitz Preserve Park has undergone numerous infrastructure facelifts. The concrete bridge that you passed under was built in 1936 to replace a wooden trestle that originally crossed the ravine. And the road you are walking on used to end at a shelter house and pergola, but they were removed in 1948 because of vandalism. To replace this facility and to provide better access, a new road was cut through the park from Admiral Way on the north boundary to a new parking lot, though you might not be able to tell that now.

> To see what happened to this new road, veer left at the first trail fork after the road narrows, and descend a short path to Schmitz Creek. (Do stop to enjoy the lovely little stream.) Cross the creek, and ascend the short flight of steps on the left.

❸ Where you crossed the creek is the site of the former parking lot. In 2002, the parks department decommissioned the road and lot and daylighted Schmitz Creek from the pipe through which it had previously flowed. The goals were to return the creek and park to a more natural setting and to rebuild the drainage to alleviate seasonal flooding. As you continue on the trail, note the many little channels you cross. Like many creeks in Seattle, Schmitz Creek does not have a single source; instead, water from numerous seeps and springs gathers in rivulets that unite to form the waterway. Because of these many sources, the trail can be muddy in the rainy season.

> From the top of the stairs, turn right, or east. You will soon cross a small footbridge over a side channel. At the next big intersection, stay right. The trail will rise a bit and then drop back toward the creek and a four-way intersection with a bench or two.

Schmitz Creek

❹ Only three parks in Seattle contain virgin forest. On the east side of the city are Seward Park and Lakeridge Park (or Deadhorse Canyon), which is slightly south of Seward. Schmitz is the third and arguably the most beautiful.

Often described as old-growth forest, it would be more correct to say that each park has old-growth characteristics. These include old and big trees. Logging did occur in Schmitz, though only in limited amounts. For the most part you are walking through a forest where many of the Douglas fir, western red cedar, and western hemlock were growing when the Denny Party arrived in 1851 and probably long before. But there is also a variety of age classes with seedlings, saplings, younger trees, and every age up to the forest giants that could be half a millennium old.

Look up and you will see another characteristic: a diverse canopy with many layers, dead snags, and numerous openings, which creates a variety of ecological niches and allows light to penetrate to the ground. And look down, or at least along the forest floor, strewn with downed dead trees and stumps. They are nurse logs, providing an ideal growing environment for the next generation of trees (particularly western hemlocks), shrubs, mosses, and ferns, as well as great habitat for bugs, birds, and mammals.

Although all three Seattle parks with first-growth trees have these characteristics, they do not have sufficient acreage to support the great diversity of old-growth forests, including many species, such as flying squirrels, marbled murrelets, and northern spotted owls, that live primarily in this ecosystem. Schmitz may not meet the full definition of an old-growth forest, but that does not detract from the incredible beauty and density of life found here; however, if you are inspired by this landscape and want to experience a fuller expression of it, then you will have to venture out of Seattle.

> Take the wide trail to the left, or east, out of the intersection. (The trail to the right takes you back to the old Schmitz Boulevard and the park entrance; the third trail goes across the creek, which you don't want to do.) Your trail will soon begin to climb the hillside. Stop when you reach a massive tree on the left with shreddy, reddish bark.

❺ Western red cedars grow slowly and steadily for up to 1,000 years and longer. Look for their buttressed bases—some in the park have 20-foot-plus circumferences—and lacy foliage. You can also find cedar stumps, some with tell-tale signs of logging, notches where loggers placed springboards for cutting above the buttresses. Because the wood is so resistant to decay, cedar stumps remain intact far longer than other local species.

Cedar trees were the most important plant to the Native people of the region. They used all parts of the tree for everything from canoes to roofing, ropes to hooks, hats to bedding. The trees were also central to the lives of settlers, particularly for shingles. For many years, Ballard crowned itself the "Shingle Capital of the World." In 1904, the town's mills produced more than 632 million shingles, or 1,202 every minute. Ballard also probably led the region in injuries; a 1903 report from Washington State's Bureau of Labor noted that 14 fingers had been lopped off at Ballard's mills in the previous two years.

Farther up the trail on the right is another classic Pacific Northwest forest tree. Red alders have gray, birch-like bark (which some people like to mar with graffiti), oval leaves with toothed margins, and, in spring, dangling catkins that produce abundant yellow pollen. The trees thrive in altered habitat because of their ability to obtain nitrogen, a critical nutrient for plant growth. Bacteria that invade the alders' roots convert, or fix, atmospheric nitrogen into a form usable by the trees. Fast growers, reaching 80 feet in 20 years, alders typically die young, at 60 to 70 years old.

Continue up the trail as it leads out of the park to a dead-end roadway, SW Hinds Street. Walk up Hinds to 49th Avenue SW.

❻ Many of the houses in the next few blocks were built as part of the post–World War II boom in Seattle. The caption of a photo of this area from the *Seattle Times* noted that one firm had completed 200 units in 1950, 75 percent of which were "bought by former G.I.s who have completed their education in recent months." Typical prices were $9,000 to $12,000.

The next several blocks are a transition that helps to create a loop that takes you back toward Puget Sound. Walk south on 49th Avenue SW, turn right, or west, on SW Spokane Street, and follow it as it angles past Schmitz Park Elementary and becomes 51st Avenue SW. Turn right, or west, at SW Charlestown and continue to just past 55th Avenue SW to where Charlestown begins to descend. Enjoy the beautiful views out to Puget Sound, the Kitsap Peninsula, Bainbridge Island, and the Olympic Mountains.

❼ Look west to see a curious geological feature on Alki Point, the high mound topped by the red apartment building and tall trees. It's between you and the water and may seem low, but it does rise 75 feet above its surroundings. (The walk will eventually go around this mound.)

Not only is it anomalously high, but it is an unusual rock. Unlike its immediate surroundings, which consist of beach sand deposited after the glacial ice receded to the north 16,400 years ago, the mound's rock is a 23- to 28-million-year-old sandstone known as the Blakeley Formation. It formed from sediments that washed off the Cascade Mountains into a marine basin and were subsequently uplifted to the surface by the Seattle Fault. (For more information, see Walk 15.)

Imagine standing where you are now during the last movement of the fault about 1,100 years ago, when the ground rose 20 feet. Prior to the earthquake, the mound would have been a seastack rising directly out of the water. Perhaps at very low tide, you could have walked across a beach to it. After the uplift though, the mound and its sandy surroundings would have been thrust up above the high-tide line to their present position.

Stay on the main road, which becomes SW Orleans Street and then Hillcrest Avenue SW, to where it intersects SW Spokane Street. Turn left, or west, walk to 59th Avenue SW, and turn left, or south.

❽ The hillside to the east along 59th has long been known for its landslides, with the earliest recorded one occurring in 1933. If you were to walk up onto the steep slopes behind the houses along 59th Avenue, you would find many places with quite soggy ground and flowing water. The landslide zone extends the entire length of the west side of the West Seattle peninsula; if the slope is steep, it's susceptible to landslides.

Continue south on 59th Avenue SW to SW Andover Street.

❾ On the southeast corner is the former Sea View Hall, built in 1904 for John and Ella Maurer. They used it as a summer cabin and also rented it out to others who desired to escape Seattle and spend part of the summer at Alki Point. Note the use of vertical logs, a style not typical in the area. The house sold in 2005 and was extensively repaired.

Continue south on 59th Avenue SW to Carroll Street.

❿ The northwest corner is the site of the former Carroll Street school, also known as "the little red schoolhouse," which opened in 1908. Kids from as far away as Luna Point at the mouth of the Duwamish River walked more than two miles over bluffs and across muddy fields to reach the school, the only one in the neighborhood until 1911. It closed in 1913.

59th Avenue becomes Chilberg Avenue SW at Carroll. Follow Chilberg as it splits into two lanes. They end at the same place, after which the united street curves west to Beach Drive SW. Turn left, or south, on Beach, and walk a short way to Me-Kwa-Mooks Park. Continue to an open field, turn left, and walk east over to a sign in the southeast corner.

⓫ Me-Kwa-Mooks is a corruption of the Whulshootseed term *sbaqWáb-aqs,* or Prairie Point. (You will sometimes see the park's name translated as "shaped like a bear's head," but this has been discredited.) In 1908, Ferdinand and Emma Schmitz built their home, named *Sans Souci,* or "without care," on the 40 acres they owned at this location. The property included fruit and nut trees, an extensive garden, a barn, and two ponds. To the north, their children built two additional homes, both of which still stand.

LANDSLIDES IN SEATTLE

Seattle is a landslide prone city. Since 1890 more than 1,500 have happened, ranging in size from small slope failures to massive slabs cascading down and taking out buildings and roads. They occur across the city, though most often on steep slopes.

Most of the slides are caused by contact between two layers deposited during the last ice age: the Lawton Clay and Esperance Sand. When rain falls in Seattle, it typically percolates down into the upper layer, the Esperance, which is relatively permeable. The Lawton, in contrast, is impermeable; when water seeps through the Esperance Sand down to the underlying very fine-grained clay, it tends to perch, or collect, at the boundary and then move laterally until it emerges at the surface as a spring or seep. It is this zone of saturated land where most of the city's landslides occur. (For more information on these layers, see the sidebar about glaciers in Walk 12.)

Me-Kwa-Mooks Park became city property through several acquisitions, including Emma Schmitz's 1945 donation of the beachfront and a 1971 purchase of the forested acres of the Schmitz property.

Carefully cross Beach Drive to the waterfront side.

⑫ Low tide (meaning 0 or lower) reveals another unusual bit of geology—low brown layers of rock rising out of the pebbles and sand. These are beds of peat deposited around 28,000 years ago, when freshwater lakes, peat bogs, forested uplands, and river valleys (or an environment similar to our modern one) covered the region. They are visible at the surface because of uplift of the Seattle Fault. If the tide is low enough, look for folds in the peat beds created by uplift along the Seattle Fault.

Walk north on Beach Drive SW about one-third mile to SW Carroll Street and Weather Watch Park, one of several wonderful pocket parks in the last mile or so of the walk.

⑬ This park is one of many street-end green spaces in Seattle that have been converted from an unloved lot to a beloved public place. From 1907 to 1920, the *Eagle* steamboat, which ferried between downtown Seattle and here, stopped at a dock on this site. Like so many abandoned lots, it moldered until someone, in this instance artist Lezlie Jane, decided to create a park space. She made sketches, held meetings, built community support, gained permission from public agencies, and raised the money to complete her vision. The project, which Jane completed in 1991, took seven years from start to finish.

Continue north on Beach Drive SW three blocks to Cormorant Cove at SW Orleans Street.

⓮ This is another one-of-a-kind park space designed by Lezlie Jane, who again secured permitting and raised the money. In 1995, the parks department bought the two-acre property formerly planned for condo development. They leveled a grocery store on the lot but didn't have money for further work, which led to the Alki Community Council asking Jane to develop a park plan. As the text around the mosaic of the cormorant notes, the key point in creating the new space was the removal of a 12-foot-high bulkhead that restricted beach access.

Continue north one block to Constellation Park and Marine Reserve at 63rd Avenue SW and Beach Drive SW.

⓯ Here again is the result of Lezlie Jane's work—the best public space in the city to learn about the constellations in the sky. Twenty-seven bronze constellations (Avenue of the Stars) are embedded in the concrete along Beach Drive. On clear nights, each depicted constellation is viewable in the sky at 10:00 p.m., but at different times of the year. In addition, the sidewalk display illustrates the planets in early December 1997, when seven of them were in alignment and visible from Earth, a phenomenon that won't happen again for about a hundred years. On a more earthly note, don't miss the winsome creatures that "inhabit" the nearby tidepool and below it the 32-foot-long tiled wall depicting intertidal marine life.

Stay along the water and continue along Beach Drive SW to 64th Avenue SW.

⓰ Additional outcrops of the Blakeley Formation rise out of the water along the beach at low tide. Because of the uplift caused by movement of the Seattle Fault, the beds of gray rock are tilted almost vertical (90 degrees) from their original horizontal position. The uplift of the Blakeley and the surrounding sands also resulted in an unusual ecosystem at Alki

Alki Lighthouse

Point: windswept and with a high water table of brackish water and less stable soils due to storm events and extreme high tides. These conditions created a prairie (hence, the name Me-Kwa-Mooks) mostly devoid of trees except for a few shore pines.

Continue on Beach Drive SW as it curves right, or north, and becomes Alki Avenue SW to the Alki Point lighthouse.

⓱ Hans Hanson, who purchased Doc Maynard's land in 1868, was the first to warn sailors of the dangers of Alki Point. He hung a brass kerosene lantern from a post on his barn. In 1887, Hanson was named the official light keeper by the US Lighthouse Board. He earned $15 a month. When Hanson died in 1900, his son and cousins continued trimming the wick, cleaning the glass, and lighting and extinguishing the lantern until 1910. The federal government built the present lighthouse in 1913 with a Fresnel lens that produced light visible for 12 miles.

As you walk around the point, note the high mound on your right. This is the high point composed of the Blakely Formation rocks.

THE "CORRECT" PRONUNCIATION OF ALKI

Al-key or *Al-kye*, that is the great pronunciation question in Seattle. Old-timers will tell you that it rhymes with tree, though few others will agree. No matter what, the word means "by and by" in Chinook jargon, the argot of the regional trade network.

Continue around Alki Point on Alki Avenue SW. Past 64th Place SW are many artworks and historical monuments, most of which have explanatory panels. (Numbered stop 18 corresponds to the beginning of artworks and monuments.) These include large pieces such as the Birthplace of Seattle obelisk and a miniature Statue of Liberty; several points along the West Seattle Cultural Trail, which continues to the Duwamish River; and many etched and inlaid stone pavers, bronze plaques, and various viewing devices. Continue on Alki to 59th Avenue SW, turn right, or south, and return to the beginning of the walk.

18 We know of the Denny Party as Seattle's founding families, but they were not the first to land at this location with plans to settle it. In July 1833, William Fraser Tolmie, a doctor and amateur botanist working for the Hudson's Bay Company, visited the point. He had been sent to see if it might make a good location for a company trading post/fort but concluded that "the unproductive soil and inconvenience of going at least one-half mile for a supply of water" made it a poor choice. Who knows how our city history might have differed if the land had been more acceptable to Tolmie. Once again, geology plays a key role in the Seattle story.

AFTERWORD

A book of walks is by nature prescriptive, telling the reader where to go and what to see. *Seattle Walks* follows that approach, but I like to think that this book is a beginning. I hope that the walks have revealed sides of Seattle that you have not known, whether they are sights you passed by every day and had not noticed or they lay undiscovered in a part of the city you had not thought to explore.

Now that you have completed all 17 walks, or at least made it to the end of this book, I encourage you to repeat walks. Take them at different times of day, in different weather, at different times of the year. A walk in Magnuson Park in summer, for example, is so different from a stroll there in winter. Different birds have settled in. Leaves reframe your views. Sunbathers dot the shoreline. Boaters ply the lake. The rich smell of flowers permeates the air. It may feel like you have never visited the park before. And in a city that is changing so rapidly, many walks in the most developed parts of Seattle have probably evolved from when you first did them.

I truly believe that few pleasures in the city are easier or simpler to pursue than walking. It is free and requires little more than the clothes on your back. All you need is a desire and willingness to get outside, explore, and use your senses. And the possibilities just in Seattle are endless—the city has more than 2,100 miles of sidewalks and pathways with another 850 miles of streets without sidewalks and 120 miles of trails in its city parks. You could wander for months and never cover the same terrain. Have fun.

SUGGESTED READING

I used a variety of primary and secondary sources during the research for this book. Following is a list of non-primary books and articles that I found helpful. I have tried to indicate when they are no longer in print or perhaps available only in libraries or online (most of the context statements are available online).

WALK 1: HISTORIC SHORELINE Although it's not available to buy (it's in libraries and online), the best account of Seattle's historic shoreline is Paul Dorpat's *Seattle Waterfront: An Illustrated History* (Seattle: Seattle City Council, 2006). Good information is also found in *Pioneer Square: Seattle's Oldest Neighborhood*, edited by Mildred Tanner Andrews (Seattle: Pioneer Square Community Association in association with University of Washington Press, 2005). Out of print but often in libraries is J. Willis Sayre's *This City of Ours* (Seattle: Seattle School District, 1936).

WALK 2: DENNY HILL Good pictures and background are in Paul Dorpat's *Now and Then* book series, published in Seattle by Tartu Publications. Diana James's *Shared Walls: Seattle Apartment Buildings, 1900–1939* (Jefferson, NC: McFarland & Company, Inc., 2012) mentions some of the apartments that popped up post-regrade. Additional material is also in Mimi Sheridan's *Belltown Historic Context Statement and Survey Report* (Seattle: City of Seattle, Department of Neighborhoods, 2007), in *Denny Triangle Historic Survey and Inventory Context Statement* (Seattle: City of Seattle, Department of Neighborhoods, 2006), and in my book *Too High and Too Steep: Reshaping Seattle's Topography* (Seattle: University of Washington Press, 2015). There is also one novel set on Denny Hill, Peter Donahue's *Madison House* (Portland: Hawthorne Books & Literary Arts, 2005).

WALK 3: DOWNTOWN ROCKS David Knoblach probably knows more than any-one about the local stone industry. In particular, good background history, as well as a list of which type of stone is used in different buildings in different cities, can be found in his article "Washington's Stone Industry: A History," *Washington Geology* 21, no. 4 (1993): 3–17. Additional information about building materials is also in my books *The Seattle Street-Smart Naturalist: Field Notes from the City* (Portland: WestWinds Press, 2005) and *Stories in Stone: Travels through Urban Geology* (New York: Walker & Co., 2009).

WALK 4: DOWNTOWN GEOGRAPHICAL TOUR Additional information about the City Datum Point (Essay 10306) and the Seattle Tower (Essay 9633) can be found at HistoryLink.org. Historian Rob Ketcherside has a tour of Seattle street clocks on his website (www.zombiezodiac.com/rob/ped/clock/map.htm; accessed Mar. 2015). For more information about the manhole covers, including a map, see my website (www.geologywriter.com/blog/street-smart-naturalist-blog/seattle-map-3-manhole-covers/).

WALK 5: DOWNTOWN MENAGERIE Jeffrey Karl Ochsner and Dennis Alan Anderson's *Distant Corner: Seattle Architects and the Legacy of H. H. Richardson* (Seattle: University of Washington Press, 2003) provides great information on the city's late-19th- and early-20th-century buildings. Ochsner also edited *Shaping Seattle Architecture: A Historical Guide to the Architects* (Seattle: University of Washington Press, 2014), which covers a wider range of time. More insights into Seattle's terra-cotta history are in *Impressions of Imagination: Terra Cotta Seattle* (Seattle: Allied Arts of Seattle, 1986), which is out of print but is usually available in libraries, as is Lawrence Kreisman's *Made to Last: Historic Preservation in Seattle and King County* (Seattle: Historic Seattle Preservation Foundation in association with University of Washington Press, 1999). And finally, Maureen R. Elenga's *Seattle Architecture: A Walking Guide to Downtown* (Seattle: Seattle Architectural Foundation, 2007) does exactly what the title says.

WALK 6: REGRADES AND THE INTERNATIONAL DISTRICT Numerous books tell the stories of the International District. Historical accounts (generally easiest to find in libraries) include *Divided Destiny: A History of Japanese Americans in Seattle* (Seattle: University of Washington Press, 1998), by David Takami; *Meet Me at Higo: An Enduring Story of a Japanese American Family* (Seattle:

Wing Luke Museum of the Asian Pacific American Experience, 2011), by Ken Mochizuki; *Seattle's International District: The Making of a Pan-Asian American Community* (Seattle: International Examiner Press, 2009), by Doug Chin; and *Jackson Street after Hours: The Roots of Jazz in Seattle* (Seattle: Sasquatch Books, 1993), by Paul de Barros. Also rich in detail is the National Register of Historic Places Nomination Form for the International District. John Okada's brilliant novel *No-No Boy* (Seattle: University of Washington Press, 2014) portrays the Nihonmachi life just after World War II. Monica Sone's *Nisei Daughter* (Seattle: University of Washington Press, 2014) recounts her childhood in the same area. Both are still in print. Although it only has a slight mention of the International District, Carlos Bulosan's *America Is in the Heart: A Personal History* (Seattle: University of Washington Press, 1973) offers great insights into Seattle's Filipino community.

WALK 7: MADISON STREET Esther Mumford's *Seattle's Black Victorians: 1852–1901* (Seattle: Ananse Press, 1980) and Quintard Taylor's *The Forging of a Black Community: Seattle's Central District, from 1870 through the Civil Rights Era* (Seattle: University of Washington Press, 1994) provide the best accounts of the area's African American settlers. Both are found in libraries. For more information on the Madison Street Cable Company and the other street trolleys, Leslie Blanchard's long out-of-print *The Street Railway Era in Seattle: A Chronicle of Six Decades* is the best source. *Madison Park Remembered* (Seattle: J. P. Thomas, 2004), by longtime resident Jane Powell Thomas, tells the story of the neighborhood. Edited by Lawrence Kreisman, *Tradition and Change on Seattle's First Hill: Propriety, Profanity, Pills, and Preservation* (Seattle: Historic Seattle Preservation Foundation, 2014) tells the amazing stories of Seattle's first premier neighborhood.

WALK 8: LAKE UNION Thaisa Way's *The Landscape Architecture of Richard Haag: From Modern Space to Urban Ecological Design* (Seattle: University of Washington Press, 2015) offers a good perspective on Gas Works Park. Howard Droker's *Seattle's Unsinkable Houseboats* (Seattle: Watermark Press, 1977), out of print but still available in libraries, is a great source for the history of houseboats and Lake Union. The *South Lake Union Context Statement* (Seattle: City of Seattle, Department of Neighborhoods, 2005) provides great details about the south end of the lake. It also includes a bibliography of additional books and articles about the neighborhood. HistoryLink.org offers an excellent cybertour of the lake (Essay 8166), which is also available as a printable walking tour.

WALK 9: LOCKS AND DISCOVERY PARK Magnolia and Ballard have active historical societies and excellent books about the local history. These include *Passport to Ballard: The Centennial Story* (Seattle: Ballard News Tribune, 1988) and *Four Bridges to Seattle: Old Ballard, 1853–1907* (Seattle: Wandrey, 1975), which are available in many local libraries. *Magnolia: Memories and Milestones* and *Magnolia: Making More Memories* are available from the Magnolia Historical Society, which published the books. You can find additional information about the locks from the Friends of Ballard Locks. An excellent book about a disturbing incident in Fort Lawton during World War II is Jack Hamann's *On American Soil: How Justice Became a Casualty of World War II* (Chapel Hill, NC: Algonquin Books of Chapel Hill, 2005).

WALK 10: GREEN LAKE TO LAKE WASHINGTON No single source addresses the terrain covered in this walk. Good online sources to search for details include historylink.org and the Seattle Parks Department's Sherwood Park History Files (www.seattle.gov/parks/history/sherwood.htm).

WALK 11: MEADOWBROOK POND AND THORNTON CREEK The best source of information about the Meadowbrook area is Valarie Bunn's website (www.wedgwoodinseattlehistory.com). Seattle Public Utilities has good information on its website about its restoration projects in the Thornton Creek Watershed.

WALK 12: MAGNUSON PARK The Seattle Parks Department webpage for Magnuson Park (www.seattle.gov/parks/magnuson/) contains a wealth of historical information, as well as links to many reports on the redevelopment of the park. Another great source is the City of Seattle Department of Neighborhoods's webpage for the Sand Point Naval Air Station Historic District (www.seattle.gov/neighborhoods/historic-preservation/historic-districts/sand-point). The best source of information about Native people in Seattle is Coll Thrush's *Native Seattle: Histories from the Crossing-Over Place,* first edition (Seattle: University of Washington Press, 2008).

WALK 13: CAPITOL HILL The best history book on the area is *The Hill with a Future: Seattle's Capitol Hill 1900–1946* (Seattle: CPK Inc, 2001), by Jacqueline B. Williams. Unfortunately, it is out of print, but if you want the story of the hill, track it down. If you are interested in the hill's many apartments, find *Shared Walls: Seattle Apartment Buildings, 1900–1939*, by Diana E. James. Another very detailed description of houses is the online National Register of Historic Places Inventory Nomination Form for the Harvard-Belmont District. The best source of information about regional Olmsted parks is *Greenscapes: Olmsted's Pacific Northwest* (Pullman, WA: Washington State University Press, 2009), by Joan Hockaday.

WALK 14: BEACON HILL *Seattle's Beacon Hill* (Charleston, SC: Arcadia, 2003), by Frederica Merrell and Mira Latoszek, is a fine source of historical information, as well as photographs. More detailed information can also be found in Caroline Tobin's *Beacon Hill Historic Context Statement* (Seattle: City of Seattle, Department of Neighborhoods, 2004).

WALK 15: RAINIER BEACH TO COLUMBIA CITY For more information on local history (and a great reference list), see Caroline Tobin's *North Rainier Valley Historic Context Statement* (Seattle: City of Seattle, Department of Neighborhoods, 2004). The National Park Service through the National Register of Historic Places has produced a similar document for Columbia City (www.seattle.gov/documents/departments/neighborhoods/historic preservation/historicresourcessurvey/context-columbia-city.pdf; accessed Feb. 23, 2015).

WALK 16: DELRIDGE AND PIGEON POINT The Delridge History Project (delridge history.org) provides thorough background on the neighborhood, as does the out-of-print *Delridge Community History* (Seattle: Seattle Parks Department, 1994), by Gail Dubrow and Alexa Berlow. If you desire to explore more stairways, check out Jake and Cathy Jaramillo's *Seattle Stairways Walks* (Seattle: Mountaineers Books, 2012).The poet Richard Hugo, who grew up in White Center south of Delridge, wrote about Youngstown and the surrounding area in his book *The Real West Marginal Way: A Poet's Autobiography* (New York: Norton, 1986).

WALK 17: WEST SEATTLE The best histories are *West Side Story* (Seattle: Robinson Newspapers, 1987), edited by Clay Eals, and Brooke Best's *Celebrating 150 Years, Architectural History of West Seattle's North End: Harbor Avenue, Alki, and South Alki* (Seattle: Brooke V. Best, 2003). Many books cover the founding of Seattle, including Murray Morgan's *Skid Road: An Informal Portrait of Seattle* (Seattle: University of Washington Press, 1982) and *Seattle: Past to Present* (Seattle: University of Washington Press, 1976), by Roger Sales. Both are opinionated and easy to read. And no one who visits the area should miss the Log House Museum, run by the Southwest Seattle Historical Society. The museum carries *West Side Story*.

ILLUSTRATION CREDITS

All maps by Jennifer Shontz, Red Shoe Design

Page 55	Photograph by the author
Page 57	*Seattle Times* image from the collection of William Creswell
Page 59	Photograph by the author
Page 60	Photograph by the author
Page 63	Photograph by the author
Page 65	Photograph by the author
Page 68, left	Photograph by Whitney Rearick
Page 68, right	Photograph by the author
Page 70	Photograph by Whitney Rearick
Page 73	Photograph by Whitney Rearick
Page 74	Photograph by the author
Page 82	Courtesy University of Washington Special Collections, UW 28214z
Page 83	Courtesy Seattle Public Library, image spl_shp_22872
Page 88	Courtesy Museum of History and Industry
Page 91	Courtesy Museum of History and Industry, Figure 1983.10.6300.1
Page 93	Courtesy Seattle Public Library, image spl_shp_15297
Page 99	Courtesy City of Seattle Municipal Archives, Figure No. 63319
Page 102	Library of Congress, Geography and Map Division
Page 105	Photograph by the author
Page 109	Copyright ©The Boeing Company, BI23810
Page 113	Photograph by Ed LaCasse
Page 114	Courtesy University of Washington Special Collections, UW 18749
Page 116	Photograph by David Johnson
Page 120	Courtesy Army Corps of Engineers, Figure 042.038.002.093
Page 121	Photograph by Aurora Santiago
Page 125	Photograph by the author
Page 128	Courtesy City of Seattle Engineering, Drawing 782-75-3
Page 132	Courtesy National Park Service, Frederick Law Olmsted National Historic Site, Figure No. 2714–38
Page 139	Courtesy City of Seattle Municipal Archives, Figure No. 44895

INDEX

ABOUT THE AUTHOR

David B. Williams is a freelance writer focused on the intersection of people and the natural world. His most recent book was *Too High and Too Steep: Reshaping Seattle's Topography*, which won the 2016 Virginia Marie Folkins Award, given by the Association of King County Historical Organizations to an outstanding historical publication. Other books include *Stories in Stone: Travels Through Urban Geology* and *The Seattle Street-Smart Naturalist: Field Notes from the City*. Williams is also co-author of *Waterway: The Story of Seattle's Locks and Ship Canal*. He lives in Seattle and continues to explore and travel through the city by foot and by bike.